A Literary Friendship

A Literary Friendship

Correspondence between

Caroline Gordon

&

Ford Madox Ford

Edited with an Introduction
by Brita Lindberg-Seyersted

The University of Tennessee Press ⌇ Knoxville

The paper used in this book meets the minimum requirements of
ANSI/NISO Z39.48-1992 (R 1997) (Permanence of Paper). The
binding materials have been chosen for strength and durability.
Printed on recycled paper.

Library of Congress Cataloging-in-Publication Data

Gordon, Caroline, 1895–1981
    A literary friendship : correspondence between Caroline Gordon
and Ford Madox Ford / edited with an introduction by Brita
Lindberg-Seyersted. — 1st ed.
        p. cm.
Includes index.
ISBN 1-57233-046-5 (cl.: alk. paper)
1. Gordon, Caroline, 1895–1981—Correspondence. 2. Women authors,
American—20th century—Correspondence. 3. Authors, English—20th
century—Correspondence. 4. Ford, Ford Madox, 1873–1939—Correspondence.
5. Editors—GreatBritain—Correspondence. 6. Critics—Great Britain—
Correspondence. I. Ford, Ford Madox, 1873–1939. II. Lindberg-Seyersted, Brita.
III. Title.
PS3513.05765 Z49   1999
813'.52—dc21
[b]   98-40213

Contents

Preface   VII

Acknowledgments   IX

Introduction   XI

A Note on the Text   XXXV

The Correspondence

    1930–1931   3

    1932   24

    1933   42

    1934–1935   64

    1936–1937   87

    1938–1939   105

Index of Names and Titles   III

~

Preface

The friendship between Caroline Gordon (1895–1981) and Ford Madox Ford (1873–1939) has figured—prominently or peripherally—in most biographical and critical treatments of these two writers; in Gordon's case, their friendship was a crucial element in her literary career, and in Ford's, it was a constant in his "American" life. The relationship between them has a sure place in twentieth-century American literary history with connections to important literary milieus of the modernist era. It therefore seems fitting to fill out the story of this relationship by presenting their correspondence to each other as fully as possible. In addition to this literary-historical value, Gordon's letters, in particular, offer other kinds of rewards: she gives vivid and often amusing insights into the life of a struggling writer, and she lets us into an unconventional atmosphere, playful and strenuous by turns, that the two writers and their respective households shared. Ford's letters preeminently bear out his reputation as a selfless helper and mentor. The letters testify to their ongoing discussion of each other's work, with the focus on literary technique.

From Gordon's hand we have a substantial cache of letters, held by Cornell University Library, while of Ford's letters to her only a minor part has survived; they are at Princeton University Library. In this material, there are references to other letters, which are now lost or missing. A few of Gordon's letters are addressed to Ford's companion Janice Biala, but they are clearly intended for Ford as well.

In order to set the letters in context, a biographical introduction will outline the most significant traits of the story behind the correspondence. Gordon very seldom dated her letters and often omitted place, and such details are also often missing in Ford's correspondence. To establish their often-shifting whereabouts and their activities, I have therefore consulted two other kinds of sources in addition to the correspondence itself: letters by Ford and Gordon and members of their families to other correspondents and biographies about my two protagonists. I have turned to *The Correspondence of Ford Madox Ford and Stella Bowen* (Bloomington: Indiana Univ. Press, 1993), carefully edited by Sondra J. Stang and Karen Cochran, for factual details of Ford's addresses as well as for his doings in the United States during the relevant period of his life. *The Southern Mandarins: Letters of Caroline Gordon to Sally Wood, 1924–1937* (Baton Rouge: Louisiana State Univ. Press, 1984), edited by Sally Wood, has provided me with intimate and lively information concerning Gordon's life as a wife and mother and her struggles to find time and energy for what her friend Andrew Lytle called "this misery of fitting words together" (letter to Allen Tate, Sept. 17, 1938). Thomas Daniel Young and Elizabeth Sarcone's edition of *The Lytle-Tate Letters: The Correspondence of Andrew Lytle and Allen Tate* (Jackson: Univ. Press of Mississippi, 1987) was of help in fixing certain dates and addresses for the migratory Tates. As for biographies I acknowledge my debt to Arthur Mizener's *The Saddest Story: A Biography of Ford Madox Ford* (New York and Cleveland: The World Publishing Company, 1971) as the basic life, and most recently to Max Saunders's two-volume *Ford Madox Ford: A Dual Life* (New York: Oxford Univ. Press, 1996), which with its wealth of scrupulous documentation complements and corrects Mizener's biography. For details about Gordon's life, I have turned to three recent biographies: Ann Waldron's *Close Connections: Caroline Gordon and the Southern Renaissance* (Knoxville: Univ. of Tennessee Press, 1987), Veronica A. Makowsky's *Caroline Gordon: A Biography* (New York: Oxford Univ. Press, 1989) with its narrower scope, and Nancylee Novell Jonza's *The Underground Stream: The Life and Work of Caroline Gordon* (Athens: Univ. of Georgia Press, 1995), which in its way is a sort of dual-life story uncovering Gordon's "demon" as well as her "genius."

Acknowledgments

I am pleased to express my gratitude to Nancy Tate Wood for permission to publish these letters by her mother, Caroline Gordon. I also thank the Division of Rare Books and Manuscript Collections at Cornell University Library for permission to bring out the letters in full. Throughout the years I have profited from the efficiency and helpfulness of curator and staff at Cornell University Library, and while preparing the present edition I have found Lucy B. Burgess's assistance to be particularly valuable. I am deeply grateful to Janice Biala for her kind permission to publish letters by Ford Madox Ford to Caroline Gordon, a couple of them with contributions from herself. I also thank her for giving me her views on matters relating to Ford during a rewarding conversation in Paris in November 1997. I am indebted to the Princeton University Library for permission to publish Ford Madox Ford's letters to Caroline Gordon, which are located in the Caroline Gordon Papers, Box 32, Folder 8, Manuscripts Division, Department of Rare Books & Special Collections, Princeton University Library. The staff at the Department of Rare Books & Special Collections, especially Reference Librarian Margaret M. Sherry, gave me excellent service.

Other libraries gave assistance of different kinds. I acknowledge permission to quote from two letters from Caroline Gordon to Katherine Anne Porter and one letter from Katherine Anne Porter to Peggy Cowley to the Papers of Katherine Anne Porter, Special Collections, University of Maryland, College Park, Libraries. From the Yale Collection of American Literature, Beinecke Rare Book and

Manuscript Library, Yale University, I received copies of letters from Caroline Gordon to Josephine Herbst; and Oslo University Library supplied me with books and articles from near and far.

I owe personal debts to my colleague Bjørn Tysdahl for his valuable comments on my project and to my husband, Per Seyersted, for always being ready to discuss my work with me. Else Bjerke Westre was of great help in preparing the final manuscript.

Introduction

The year 1926 was an important one in the story of the literary friendship between Caroline Gordon and Ford Madox Ford. It was also a decisive one in Ford's long and eventful career as a writer: Ford, the British artist-gentleman, took action to establish himself more securely and permanently as an important actor on the American literary scene. He had behind him a long and distinguished career as a writer, as an editor, and, in general, as a highly visible actor in the literary world. Born into a large family of practitioners of the arts with an international flavor—he was a son of the German-born musicologist Francis Hueffer and related to the Pre-Raphaelite Rossettis[1]—he started out as the young author of a fairy tale, *The Brown Owl* (1891). This was followed up by a long series of poems, novels, and critical and biographical writings. His novel *The Good Soldier* (1915), narrating the story of four people caught in a web of love, betrayal, and tragedy, and the trilogy *The Fifth Queen* (1906–8), with Katharine Howard, one of Henry VIII's eight wives, as a main character, have been highly praised—the first for its psychological insight and its literary technique, the other for the skill with which historical personages are made to come alive to the modern reader. His editorship of the *English Review* (1908–9) was one of the highlights of his life, as was his editorship of the Paris-based *transatlantic review* (1924). Shortly before his entry into the American scene (1924–26), he had published three of the four novels that were later gathered into one unit, *Parade's End* (1950). This was Ford's truly impressive recreation of the end of an era, with the Great War as the focal event, and the transition to a new world and a new mentality.

These *literary* successes were, however, accompanied by matrimonial problems and poor health, partly due to his participation in the war, as well as economic shortages, even disasters, and by 1926 it seemed to him that he needed a change of scene. He had come to realize—or at least to believe—that his future prospects of success lay in the United States, for his books were selling better there than in Great Britain, and New York, rather than London, was now a center of energy and initiative. New York was the place where the money was, and where the most influential people were gathered. Paris was and would always remain his favorite city, but after the collapse of his great editing venture, the *transatlantic review*, the French capital no longer offered the same fertile field for his passions as a man of letters.

Accordingly, on October 20, 1926, Ford sailed for the United States with a lecture tour as the most immediate program. The main purpose was, as his biographer Arthur Mizener says, "to work on his new American career."[2] He wrote home to his companion Stella Bowen about the overwhelming reception that reporters and other New Yorkers gave him and about his own response to the Big Apple: he "really like[d] it very much indeed."[3] At first his friends, the writer Herbert Gorman and his wife Jean, took him in, but he soon found an apartment at 51 West 16th Street, not very far from their place. He didn't like his apartment—it was in "a great, gloomy old house" (F–B 240)—but it was quiet and evidently conducive to work, for he began at once to produce articles, essays, and lectures intended to boost his reputation and augment his sparse financial resources.

On December 21 Ford reports: "I have got a young woman in to dictate to in the mornings—and am going to begin the articles for Harper's . . ." (F–B 268). This young woman was thirty-one-year-old Caroline Gordon, wife of poet Allen Tate, mother of toddler Nancy, and journalist with literary ambitions. Exactly when and how, at the end of 1926, the two first met is, to my knowledge, unrecorded, but new contacts were surely easily made in the highly sociable and mutually supportive and interdependent literary-artistic crowd that gathered in Greenwich Village in the 1920s.

Caroline Gordon's roots were in the American South, with Kentucky and Tennessee providing social and cultural nurture. This meant an immersion in the history of the South, especially the tragedy of the Civil War; close ties to many branches of the family, the "Connection"; and respect for an old type of education where the classics were a self-evident part. Two people were particularly important to her. One was her grandmother, Caroline Ferguson Meriwether, whose place in Kentucky, Merry Mont, always offered housing and security. The other was her father, James Maury Morris Gordon, who may have transmitted to her the "migratory" bug: he moved himself and his family from place to place, and he shifted occupation more than once, until he evidently accepted the pre-ordained role of "sportsman" that his daughter later gave him in a book based on his life.

Gordon had arrived in Greenwich Village already in the fall of 1924 in pursuit of a literary career. Together with her husband (they got married in the spring of the following year), she moved about a bit, ending up again in New York in the late fall of 1926. The Tates' household in the Village has received a prominent place in the annals of several writers, and commentators have delivered colorful descriptions of the inhabitants, their friends, and transitory houseguests. Josephine Herbst, a writer-friend of the Tates, reminisced: "Allen Tate and Caroline Gordon held out in a basement apartment on Bank Street with rent free in return for janitor service. Allen stoked the furnace, while Caroline looked after the stairs and hallways, hiring neighborhood colored women to scrub and clean."[4] Mizener describes the legendary house: "Twenty-seven Bank Street was a small, three-story building in which the Tates had two and a half basement rooms, the half room being regularly occupied by friends such as Katherine Anne Porter, Robert Penn Warren, and Andrew Lytle" (Mizener 359). In a letter to Bowen Ford was later to commiserate with the Tates on their living conditions:

> But the way those people live is something terrible. They are the janitors in a big apartment house—for wh. they get two rooms and nothing, and have to do all the concierge's work. Then they make $18 a week by letting one room and that is all they have except an occasional dollar or so for a review. And Tate is such a nice fellow and a good poet and she extraordinarily well educated and quite a lady—from the S[outh]. However, they seem fairly cheerful—for tho' their basement is dreadfully damp there is quite a largish garden for N.Y. . . . anyhow my taking her on is quite a godsend for them too (F–B 341; Ford's ellipsis).

Allen Tate, however, remembered this period of janitorship as far from marked by poverty and squalor. He told Mizener that "Never since that time have I felt so well off" (Mizener 359). Gordon, the conservative southern lady, supported herself by taking diverse jobs, such as proofreading and working as a typist for the American Society for Cultural Relations with Russia. As a secretary for Ford that winter of 1926–27, her task was to type various pieces he dictated to her. On December 22 he wrote to Bowen: "I shall have to break off now for the young person.—Mrs. Allen Tate who passes as Miss—Gordon—who writes for me has arrived" (F–B 272), and on December 31 he finished dictating to her a tribute to Ezra Pound (F–B 281): his review of *Personae: The Collected Poems of Ezra Pound* ("Ezra"), which appeared in the *New York Herald Tribune Books* on January 9, 1927.[5] On January 3, 1927, he began dictating his "new book" (F–B 284). This was *New York Is Not America* (published in 1927), not *Last Post* (published in 1928), as has been assumed.[6] Gordon evidently took her job quite seriously. Two days after Ford began dictating the new book to her, he slept late into the morning—so he confesses to Bowen—and was awakened by his secretary "making horrible noises with the buzzer that takes the place of a doorbell" (F–B 286).

For a brief, glorious moment Ford was something of a celebrity in New York, and he loved it. Douglas Goldring, a one-time subeditor of Ford's *English Review*, witnessed his success. "It was evident," he writes in his reminiscences, "that [Ford] adored New York and that New York—or, at least, its literary circles—had responded by taking him to its hospitable bosom. Probably for the first time in his life he found himself accepted as a Great Man."[7] A young bookshop assistant (later journalist), Calvin Fixx, told a friend, in some awe, how one day he had practically rubbed shoulders with Ford.[8] But it was not only the young who feted him: in December he was a guest of honor at a P.E.N. Club dinner (F–B 263, 268).

Soon, however, this pleasurable part of Ford's American errand was broken off, for he was scheduled to go to Chicago in January to lecture. He was invited for dinner to Hemingway's parents' home in fashionable Oak Park. Dr. Hemingway found Ford to be "a very charming guest" (quoted in Mizener 355). The Midwest was not to Ford's liking, however. He thought it was depressing and didn't wonder that "all the women" in the stories of its writers "go mad or to the bad" (F–B 300). The literary world of America was small indeed; so, for example, at a tea party in Chicago, Glenway Wescott, whom Ford had known in Paris and who was to become a close friend of Katherine Anne Porter, was also present.

At the end of February it was time for Ford to return to Europe, but not before he had given a farewell tea party. Gordon, his helper, counted sixty-six guests (F–B 320). Not wanting to let go of the momentum his appearances at various American scenes had created during the past winter, he was back in New York already in the fall of 1927. On board ship, so he recorded the event, he finished *Last Post,* the last volume of the tetralogy *Parade's End* (F–B 321). Things had changed somewhat in the Village. The building where he had stayed the year before, 51 West 16th Street, was now being pulled down, so he resided at the National Arts Club at 15 Gramercy Park, a very decent address. Soon he was in touch with the Tates again; he invited them for lunch and reengaged "Miss Gordon (Mrs Tate)" as his secretary (F–B 340). She began this new stint on October 29. The arrangement was for Ford to go to 27 Bank Street, to dictate to her there. Her first job was to type his novel about Marshal Ney, that is, *A Little Less Than Gods,* to be serialized in *Collier's Weekly.* (The serialization deal came to nothing.) On November 16 he wrote to Bowen: ". . . setting out for my office—which is what 27 Bank St amounts to . . ." (F–B 354). This set-up was naturally awkward, and by November 29 he gave his address as 27 Bank Street. He was pleased with his quarters on the second floor: "It is a beautifully bright room in a very old sort of Bloomsbury street" (F–B 360). His secretary screened incoming phone calls; she "only interrupts me when she judges it necessary— which works pretty well." According to Mizener, Ford even took his meals with the Tates. Evidently the fare was not always up to French *déjeuner* standards; once he was offered "a poached egg & some grapes" for lunch (F–B 362).

Having renewed contacts with Ford, it was now the Tates' turn to benefit from the arrangement. Ford recommended Tate for a Guggenheim Fellowship, with good results—he received a grant for 1928. Ford also tried to find a British publisher for his poems. Tate responded by subtitling his 1928 biography of Stonewall Jackson "the Good Soldier," alluding to Ford's experimental novel of 1915 and to his well-earned reputation as a tireless and undaunted champion of good writing. Trusting to Ford's benevolent interest in younger writers' work, Gordon showed him a story she had recently completed, "Old Mrs. Llewellyn." Apparently he was not enthusiastic, but he offered a kind but noncommittal "Humph, that's ver' nice."[9]

After the Stonewall Jackson biography had appeared in May 1928, the Tates' whereabouts and activities were to some extent guided by Tate's next project, which was a biography of Jefferson

Davis, president of the Confederacy. It took them on a camping trip south in the summer to visit Civil War battlefields. For some time in 1928 they stayed at 561 Hudson Street, a famous address among New York intelligentsia and bohemians. Katherine Anne Porter was also a member of the group. The place, which had been the headquarters of a West Side gang, was named Casa Caligari after a well-known horror movie.

Then it was time for the Tates to sail for Europe. They went via England, stopping off in London for Tate to use the libraries, and in Oxford, where their close friend Robert Penn Warren was spending the year on a Rhodes scholarship. After two months of traveling, they arrived in Paris, their prime goal, in late November 1928. They settled at the Hôtel Fleurus, recommended to them by Caroline's friend Sally Wood. The hotel was conveniently close to Ford's apartment at 32 rue de Vaugirard. He eagerly acted as the friendly adviser, persuading them to remain in Paris for the winter instead of going south, as Caroline had wanted to do.

When Ford returned to Paris in early 1928, having spent the winter of 1927–28 in America, he and Stella Bowen broke up amicably, partly because he had formed an attachment to an American lady, Rene Wright. Stella had secured a separate flat for him at 32 rue de Vaugirard. In May he was back in New York. Now, to complicate matters drastically, he became involved in a relationship with yet another American woman, the young Elizabeth Cheatham. (Max Saunders is the first biographer to make full use of the material documenting this relationship.)[10]

By the fall Ford was again in Paris, ready to welcome the Tates. Having lost Stella and being far from his newest American love, he was in great need of company, and the Tates became regular and appreciative guests at his Saturday soirees. Tate reminisced how they "sat at the feet of the master; Ford, however, talked little but rather nodded agreement or disagreement."[11] That was in 1928. "But in the autumn of 1929," Tate continues,

> the *soirées* became much more literary and tyrannously competitive. We were commanded to play a difficult French parlor game called *bouts-rimés*. Ford passed around pencils and paper and assigned us the rhyme words of a Shakespeare sonnet or of a sonnet by "my aunt Christina Rossetti, a beautiful poet." Everybody had to use the assigned rhymes, and the winning sonnet was graded on both its quality and the speed of its composition. Ford himself usually won and gave as a second prize a melancholy-looking round cake which was sliced at once and eaten with moderate zest by the company.

Ever since his prewar affair with the novelist Violet Hunt (1862–1942), Ford had in vain tried to persuade his wife to agree to a divorce. He had married the young Elsie Martindale in 1894. In spite of his love for his two daughters, he wished to break out of this marriage. By the end of January 1929, when he left for New York, he still had not given up hope of prevailing on Elsie to grant him his hotly desired divorce.[12] The Tates and their friend Léonie Adams, a poet who was also in Europe on a Guggenheim, moved into his tiny apartment at 32 rue de Vaugirard. They lived there rent-free in exchange for Gordon's services: she retyped a five-hundred-page manuscript, correcting the mistakes made by a French typist who had converted every e into an a, and who had supplied every inanimate object with sex, as Gordon told Josephine Herbst.[13] Gordon was delighted with the apartment and its very Parisian view. Tate describes it in his memoirs: "[Ford's] flat consisted of a *petit salon* furnished with a divan which, like that of the typist in 'The Waste Land,' became at night a bed; this room, in the British phrase, was the bed-sitting room of my wife and me. At the far end was a small room with a small bed occupied by our daughter; near the entrance a narrow closet was just large enough for Miss Adams" (*Memoirs* 48–49). Stella Bowen and daughter Julie lived in another flat at the same address. This was when she painted a portrait of the Tates showing three rather morose-looking people without any close ties that might make them a unity. In a letter to Sally Wood, Gordon describes the portrait as she saw it in the summer of 1929: "Allen and I, held together in space, by Nancy, as it were."[14]

After bouts with Parisian grippe and periods of flagging inspiration for their respective literary projects, the Tates spent an enjoyable vacation in Brittany. (Their stay there found its way into one of Gordon's novels, *Aleck Maury, Sportsman* [1934], where Maury thinks of his daughter and her scholar-husband on a vacation in Brittany.) Then came time for them to return to Paris to hand over the keys of his flat to Ford and to get installed at the Hôtel de la Place de l'Odéon, and to pick up again the routine of dinners at Ford's establishment and evenings in his company at such famous haunts as Au Nègre de Toulouse, the Deux Magots, and the Closerie des Lilas. Literary celebrities such as Fitzgerald, Hemingway, and the formidable Miss Stein contributed to making life interesting.

Ford was no doubt desperate for company, having had to give up all hope of ever getting a divorce from Elsie. Rene Wright had all the time insisted on marriage, and young Elizabeth had gotten married in the spring of 1929 (Saunders 2: 359), so now Ford was without an intimate female companion, a situation apparently unbearable to him. In Veronica A. Makowsky's scenario, Ford "proposed" to Caroline Gordon "in a Parisian church."[15] Whatever his terms of appeal may have been in claiming affection from a woman he admired, surely they cannot have been intended nor interpreted as a serious proposal of marriage, since Elsie had slammed shut the door to his freedom forever, and Gordon was deeply attached to her husband. But, as his letters to her in the early months of 1930 show, before he met his last love, Janice Biala, his loneliness drove him to fantastic plans for a life at least in Gordon's nearness *(FMF 2, 3,* and *4).*[16]

The year 1929 marked the beginning of Gordon's literary career. In November her first publication, the short story "Summer Dust," appeared in a mimeographed magazine published by Yvor Winters. Grateful for Ford's great interest in her literary efforts, she showed him her story "Funeral in Town." She was a bit annoyed by his reaction, which took the form of hoped-for praise but ended with the remark: "Of course you don't really know what you've done."[17] Still, always helpful, he offered to try to sell the story for her. Several times he had asked to see the novel she was working on, and at the very end of the Tates' stay in Paris, she finally turned to him for an impartial assessment of her unfinished manuscript. This was what she needed: a soul mate's personal interest in her and a mentor with a passion for literature. She described the scene— and the turning point in her career—in a letter to Sally Wood:

> Our last days in Paris were very hectic. Christmas came on, with lots of gayeties and I was carousing of nights and working all day on my novel for the last three or four weeks. . . . Ford took me by the scruff of the neck about three weeks before I left, set me down in his apartment every morning at eleven o'clock and forced me to dictate at least five thousand words, not all in one morning, of my novel to him. If I complained that it was hard to work with everything so hurried and Christmas presents to buy he observed "You have no passion for your art. It is unfortunate" in such a sinister way that I would reel forth sentences in a sort of panic. Never did I see such a passion for the novel as that man has. I have known him for several years, and he has been hounding me to show him my novel all that time. But you know I never have anything in a state to show anybody. And besides I never thought he would like it. I did show him some short things which I myself rather fancied, some of them a damn sight better done than the novel, and he would mumble in his moustache "Beautiful writing, but I don't know what it is all about." Then finally I drags this novel, only half finished over, and he flies into a

> great rage and accuses me of concealing it from him until
> there is no time to do anything and so on and so on. I left
> the manuscript, half finished, with him, and he is going to
> try to get me a contract and an advance on it. I have no great
> hopes, however. It is hard to do anything with a half finished
> manuscript. Anyhow I am settling down in this very apart-
> ment [in New York] to try to finish it before we go to the
> country. (*Mandarins* 51–52; ellipsis in the text)

Ford's concern with Gordon's novel, *Penhally*, did not stop here. In a letter written shortly after the Tates' return to America, he followed up his early response with even stronger language, describing the shock he received on reading it—a shock of "delight" *(FMF 1)*.

The Tates had sailed for home on December 28, 1929. A poet from Chicago, Polly Chase Boyden, had given a farewell party for them, offering a very strong punch brewed by Ford.[18] Shortly after their arrival in New York they put up in "a two by four furnished apartment" at 364 West Twenty-sixth Street (*Mandarins* 50). New York was "terrible," Gordon complained to her friend Sally, and she missed the streets and squares of Paris. By March they were staying at Merry Mont, Gordon's grandmother's place in Kentucky. Things were brightening up: Gordon received an advance on her novel thanks to another influential champion of hers, Maxwell Perkins *(FMF 3)*, and Tate's prosperous brother Ben helped them acquire an eleven-room antebellum house situated on the Cumberland River in Tennessee, close to the Kentucky border. They had for a long time been hankering for a place of their own in the country, and this promised to be their dream place. The house was in great need of repair, and Gordon's father named it "Ben's Folly," which became "Benfolly." One of the outbuildings was a cottage, which Gordon thought would fit Katherine Anne Porter's needs and tastes. Tate did a swift sketch of the "beautiful place" in a letter to his friend Andrew Lytle: "a pioneer frame, dog-run hall, chimneys at end, a long ell in rear—eleven rooms; 185 acres."[19] Sally Wood came down for a first visit, and she tells how this space was used. The long dining room "was the gathering place of the household not only for meals but between them. Caroline's desk was at the Cumberland side. In the center the long table made a convenient place for manuscripts to be laid down—temporarily, of course. The fireplace heat reached far enough for quite a few people to gather around. Later, it was agreed that the room resemb[l]ed a Paris café" (*Mandarins* 56).

In the fall of 1930 Ford made another of his brief trips to America,

and Gordon invited him down to Benfolly, enticing him with ex-
pectations of good weather and work to be discussed *(CG 1)*. And
he came down in mid-October in the company of their common
friend Sue Jenkins Brown and Harold Loeb—the "model" for
Hemingway's character Robert Cohn—and Loeb's girlfriend. "We
had a grand time," Gordon wrote to Sally Wood, "going in swimming—we had several balmy days when it was enjoyable—drinking corn liquor and talking." Ford brought photos of Janice Biala.
Caroline "liked her face," she told Sally. Janice "looked like a gal
who could do without fine clothes if it should be necessary. . . ."
They all went to Nashville to lend support to Ford, who gave a
talk during a "terrible tea" at a woman's club, followed by "an even
more terrible dinner." At Benfolly Ford again acted the strict master, going over the manuscript of *Penhally* in detail, "which kept
me pretty tired all the time," she complained. She had little faith
in Ford's idea of turning *Penhally* into a trilogy, using his own pat-
tern for the *Fifth Queen* trilogy or the *Parade's End* tetralogy *(Mandarins* 61–63).

  Penhally was published in September 1931, and Gordon immediately sent off a copy to her benefactor. He graciously acknowledged the gift but grumbled gently about the fact that it was not
dedicated to him *(FMF 5)*. In her reply, she expressed her profound regrets that she had not done so *(CG 2)*. She was apologetic
about her work, and Ford's praise of it in an essay appearing in the
December issue of the *Bookman* delighted her. He "hauled off and
wrote a swell piece on 'Penhally,'" she told Sally *(Mandarins* 96).
Ford starts off with a personal declaration. "Mrs. Tate's book,
Penhally," he writes, "is a phenomenon for which I have long
waited." Then he places it in a long line of other new American
works of "a refreshing and admirable vigour." After several paragraphs he is back at *Penhally*, admitting that he uses this work as
"the peg on which to hang this dissertation on the birth of a na-
tion." It is less, he claims, because he thinks it is "the best con-
structed novel that modern America has produced than because it
has occasioned [him] to have these thoughts." *Penhally* is "a work
of great composure and tranquillity," serving to deal with "the tragedy of a race and the disappearance of a deeply in-bitten civilization." As for its excellent construction, "every word of it leads on
to the appointed end. Its themes are woven and interwoven, the
story [of a house in the Old South and generations of its inhabit-
ants] progresses forward in action and back in memory so that the
sort of shimmer that attaches to life attaches also to the life of the

book."[20] In response to Ford's praise of the form of the novel, she gratefully acknowledged her very direct debt to him in this respect. She was overjoyed to receive praise from someone whose judgment she most respected *(CG 4)*.

Ford had praised the opening sentence of *Penhally*. The book begins like this: "The shadows that laced the gravelled walk shifted and broke and flowed away beneath his boot soles like water." Ford's assessment was not shared by another reader: Gordon's father. He thought that the first sentence was "deadly dull." Gordon was amused by his comments and sent them along to Ford, expressing her amazement that her father had actually enjoyed the novel after he got over that first dull hurdle.[21]

The publication of Gordon's first novel evidently worked in her favor, for in March 1932 she was awarded a Guggenheim Fellowship. In a letter of February 28, 1932, she alerted Ford to her arrival in France at the end of the summer, to stay "somewhere where it's warm." She couldn't live through another chilly Paris winter with bouts of grippe laying the family low, she told him *(CG 5)*.

It was not only in his role as literary mentor that Gordon appreciated Ford. Preparing her friend Sally for what to expect if she were to accompany the Tates to France, Gordon told her that she really liked being in his company: "To have even one person sort of planning things so you can get your work done helps a lot." Reassuring her friend about Ford's presumed "tyrannies," Gordon had this to say referring to the Tates' stay in Paris in 1929: "Really, he never did anything worse than demand that we spend all our evenings with him at a period when he was undergoing all sorts of terrific troubles (a fool doctor had told him he was likely to kick off any minute)." This time, Gordon hoped, it would be his new companion, the painter Janice Biala, who would bear the brunt of his "mild tyrannies" *(Mandarins* 100).

Ford and Biala had met in Paris on May Day, 1930. She had come to one of his "Thursday teas" in the hope of meeting Ezra Pound (Mizener 393). From then on she was to be Ford's most devoted and loving supporter, who was willing to share whatever slings and arrows that arrogant publishers and ungrateful ex-friends aimed at an aging man of letters with health and money problems. Born in Biala, a town in Russian Poland, she had immigrated in 1913 to America, where she studied art. As an artist she took the name of her home town instead of her family name, Tworkov (originally Tworkovski). When she met Ford, she was just starting a distinguished career as a painter in America and in France.[22]

Both Ford and Biala loved the culture of the Mediterranean, and in March 1931 they had a stroke of luck: they found a place in Toulon, the Villa Paul on Cap Brun, which answered their idea of decent living. For some time now Ford was to shuttle between Toulon and Paris, where he kept up a pied-à-terre. Having spent the winter in Paris, they returned to the Villa Paul in the early spring of 1932, leaving their flat at 32 rue de Vaugirard in the hands of Katherine Anne Porter and her husband-to-be, Eugene Pressly *(FMF 7)*. When the Tates arrived in Paris at the end of July, it was their turn to benefit from Ford's helpfulness, and they moved into his flat for a brief spell while he was abroad, visiting Pound in Rapallo. Later on in August the Tates and Sally Wood drove down to Toulon, where they at first stayed at the Villa Paul. Gordon met Biala for the first time. With her sharp pen— as sharp as her tongue could be—she sketched her new acquaintance in a letter to Léonie Adams, who had been a member of their party during their previous stay in France: "She is a Russian Jew. More Russian than Jew. Slavic eye and Slavic melancholy and a Jewish way of making herself unpopular. She is a fine gal, though, and sticks to Ford through thick and thin. Dotes on him, in fact. We distressed her often by our lack of reverence."[23] Gordon's view of Biala seems, for a long time, to have been characterized by this mixture of standoffishness and sincere admiration for Biala's wholehearted commitment. In a personal crisis later in life, she benefited from Biala's loyalty and efficiency.

The Villa Paul was not suited for such a large company, and the Tates were eager to find a place of their own. "Ford," Allen complained to Andrew Lytle, "has behaved very badly—insisted that we visit him in his villa where it was impossible to sleep or work; but at last I won the battle, and got away" (L–T 63). Gordon was equally explicit about the precarious situation of sharing house and household at the Villa Paul. "Getting away from the Ford hospitality was an effort!" she confided to Katherine Anne Porter. "They were starved for companionship and had it all planned that we should stay there with them a month and then stay on another month while they went up to Paris," she went on. As for the cramped quarters, there was "no room even to take out one's tooth brush and no water to brush one's teeth if one had taken it out. . . ."[24] After they had moved to the nearby Villa les Hortensias, they still kept up the sociable routine with Ford and Biala. Sally Wood writes: "Every night either the Fords came over to our villa, we went to theirs, or we all visited a restaurant together. The talk was constantly about novel writing" (*Mandarins* 120). Ford was a born master of ceremonies, taking them to meet a British painter in a village above Cagnes-sur-Mer, and to a picnic at Cassis, commemorated by Tate in his poem "The Mediterranean," first called "Picnic at Cassis." The picnic was "perfect to the last detail," Caroline testified in her letter to Katherine Anne. One unpleasant accident darkened the sky temporarily: while the Tates were "protecting" the Villa Paul during one of Ford's and Biala's absences (probably in September), his treasured chickens were killed one night, by whom or what never came to light *(CG 9* and *10).*

Delightful as le Midi was, in November the Tates headed north, the ostensible reason being Tate's need for a good library to do research for his historical project (a biography of the Confederate general Robert E. Lee). Back in Paris they found a ground-floor studio at 37 rue Denfert-Rochereau. The studio was certainly on the primitive side, as Gordon emphasized in a letter to Sally Wood: "It's a studio . . . a long good sized room with the tiny kitchen and a balcony bedroom. . . . We're in a back court; the house in front has been done over and is pretty swell but this back part is quite unimproved—no running water and one of those stand up affairs for cabinet. There is a gas stove, though, thank God" (*Mandarins* 122). She liked the place, but even so, the studio turned out to be too uncomfortable, and by December they were installed at the Hôtel Fleurus, a move that freed her of household duties. This was a boon for a Guggenheim Fellow. There was no dearth of company available, especially after Katherine Anne Porter returned from her voluntary exile in Basel, where she had been awaiting a decision on where her husband-to-be Eugene Pressly would next be posted. The two couples had Christmas Eve dinner together at the Cochon au Lait, after which they went to friends to trim the Christmas tree, and on New Year's Day they visited the Jardin des Plantes.

Ford and Biala were also soon due in Paris. Biala's Christmas present to Gordon, her painting *The Castle of the Good King René,* served to keep the memory of their visit to Provence alive. Stella Bowen gave the Tates the portrait of them she had painted in 1929. When Ford and Biala, in early January 1933, arrived in Paris, they settled in the studio at 37 rue Denfert-Rochereau that the Tates had vacated earlier. They didn't mind the primitive living conditions, probably being at heart more bohemian than the Tates.

Both the Tates and the Presslys had been apprehensive about having to cope with Ford's poor health and worrying financial problems and Biala's pessimistic outlook. Gordon explained to Sally Wood:

> We had all been saying darkly—including Miss Porter
> (she insists on being called Mrs. Porter but I can never re-
> member), well, Miz Porter having a touch of grippe and
> being pretty crabby kept saying that if the Fords were in a
> difficult or complaining mood she for one was going to see
> little of them, a statement concurred in heartily by Col. Tate,
> and Miss Gordon, I must say, was wondering how much
> she would stand for—but they arrived most cheerful and
> we all went to lunch at the Pate D'Or and got very tight and
> then they came here to dinner at the Fleurus and praised
> the cooking, saying how unlike it was to the Mon Reve, a
> remark hastily passed over in the general good fellowship.
> (*Mandarins* 129)

The Mon Rêve was a pension near Toulon with a restaurant that
they all had been frequenting, no doubt at Ford's suggestion.

Both Gordon and Biala were outspoken women, quick at sharp-
tongued repartees. This may explain why Katherine Anne Porter, as a
comparative outsider to the group, could write of Gordon's relationship to Biala in the following way: "[Ford's] newest wife with whom
Caroline Tate carries on a bitter feud and tries to drag me in. . . ." She
herself, she insisted, had refused to be involved, giving as her reason
that she had "been dragged by experts and can't be had anymore—"[25]
One reason Porter may not have wished to enter into any argument
was that at this time Biala was painting her portrait, a portrait that the
Tates—between them—called "Battling Porter." Gordon describes it
thus: "A stout, washerwomanish woman sitting in a corner, her mitts
poised almost as if for action. If there were only another figure with a
sponge and a towel it would be perfect" (*Mandarins* 134). If this is how
the portrait came out, it certainly did not resemble the beautiful, frail-
looking Katherine Anne!

Ford's money problems had become acute when his publisher ran
away with part of his firm's money, with the result that payments to
Ford stopped. "Ford, faced with privation," Gordon wrote, "has got
very hoity toity—poor devil. Janice told K. A. he walks the floor at
night and pictures Julie [his daughter by Stella Bowen] starving. It is
at times like these that it is very difficult for his friends to rally round
him" (*Mandarins* 135).

In spite of grippe, cold weather, and problems of various kinds,
the Tates and their friends were able to get some work done. Ford,
as usual, was helpful to Gordon by offering constructive criticism
of a story she was working on. He wished for more action in the
story, and she saw the point but was more interested in character
than in action, as she told Sally Wood (*Mandarins* 137). This was

"Old Red," which turned out to be her most successful story. Ford also tried to get a wealthy man to donate a sum of money to the Tates (Saunders 2: 541n. 27). The Tates did him a good turn by helping to sell his article on Galsworthy, who had just died, to Maxwell Perkins in New York (*Mandarins* 138).

In mid-February the Tates suddenly decided to return home. Disturbing news had reached them of problems with the plumbing at Benfolly and unexpected and urgent tax claims. Since Benfolly was rented out till the summer, they headed for Merry Mont. Gordon was quick to tell Ford of her whereabouts, and, in a letter of February 27, 1933, she appealed to him for help in securing the English rights to *Penhally (CG 15)*. Some time during the summer, she responded to an idea proposed or hinted at by Ford: to undertake an assessment of his oeuvre in the vein of the pamphlet on Pound that Ford had organized and contributed to. *The Cantos of Ezra Pound: Some Testimonials,* with contributions by Hemingway, Eliot, Joyce, and others, was sent out in March 1933 in connection with the publication of an American edition of *A Draft of XXX Cantos.* Using Ford's words of praise for Pound the poet—"At once there are beauty and emotion and excitement"[26]—Gordon gives her reason why she cannot undertake such a task: she has for long been too much under his influence and has "felt too keenly the beauty and emotion and excitement" of his writing to be able to do such a thing *(CG 19)*.

By September 1933 the Tates were back at Benfolly, "dug in for the winter," as Gordon told Ford *(CG 20)*. In the same letter she told about the project she had just begun: her father's biography, which was to be "in the guise of fiction." She called it *The Life and Passion of Alexander Maury.* She liked working on this book, she said; it was "rather like knitting." She was intent on experimenting with timing, wishing to make it read "as fast as a novel."

Gordon finished this novel, which the publishers retitled *Aleck Maury, Sportsman,* by July the following year. It was published in October and bore a simple dedication: "To Ford Madox Ford." In a letter to Ford she was defensive and apprehensive, fearing that he would not like the book. She might have been able to make "a really good book out of it" if she "hadn't been so harried" *(CG 22)*. Ford praised her work, calling it "a quiet monologue addressed to someone that one likes very much and feels completely at home with." On a second reading he found even more to commend, comparing it to Turgenev's *Sportsman's Sketches.* It was "a poem rather than a novel" *(FMF 11 and 12)*. In a later letter Gordon filled in about her own view of the book. She herself saw it as a novel, not as a documentary piece on fishing: it was about how a man "made one thing triumph over everything else in his life." And she countered his underlying argument that her book lacked drama: "Isn't that drama?" But she thought she should have given her protagonist more "complications" in his life *(CG 25)*. A couple of years later Ford renewed his praise of the novel, calling it—in a letter to Allen Tate—"an exquisitely beautiful piece of work."[27]

Ford reciprocated Gordon's gesture of homage by dedicating his new book *Provence* to the Tates, referring lovingly to their visit to Toulon and the Cassis picnic: "To Caroline Gordon who chronicles another South and to Allen Tate who came to Provence and there wrote to 'that sweet land' the poem called 'The Mediterranean' and where we went in the boat was a long bay." Gordon thought the dedication was "lovely" and wrote that they were "very proud" *(CG 25)*. Allen Tate, in his turn, dedicated his collection *The Mediterranean and Other Poems* (1936) to Ford, "who gave me the poem."

Ford and Biala had spent most of the years 1933 and 1934 in their beloved Villa Paul, but by the end of 1934 it had seemed urgent to make a reappearance on the American scene. Gordon was doubtful about the wisdom of such a reappearance, as she told Sally Wood. She feared that he had not been away long enough "for his misdeeds to die out in the public, or rather the literary clique mind . . ." (*Mandarins* 169). She may have been thinking of the stir created by Violet Hunt's *I Have This to Say* (1926), a book in which Hunt poured out her resentment of Ford's behavior toward her, or of the rumors about his most recent entanglements with American ladies, or, again, Gordon may have had in mind Ford's frequent hassles with publishers. She herself would be glad "to see the two critters." Anyway, by November Ford and Biala were back in New York. They found an apartment at 61 Fifth Avenue and settled in for the winter. Christmas Day was spent with Ford's old friend Theodore Dreiser at Mount Kisco. In the spring of 1935 Ford again saw the Tates. They had suggested he join them for a writers' conference in Baton Rouge on April 10–11. One of the purposes of this conference was to announce the founding of the *Southern Review*, planned to represent the views and interests of the Southern Agrarians. After giving a lecture at Southwestern College in Memphis, where Allen Tate was now teaching, Ford traveled with the Tates to Baton Rouge. At the conference he appeared as a promoter of women writers, among them Gordon. There were disagreements as well: Ford and Gordon did not see eye to eye on the role of the northern literary establishment. He thought that southern writers were in no way discriminated against by the New York literary establishment. In a letter to daughter Julie (May 22, 1935), Ford boasted of making "a speech lasting two hours and a quarter to the University of Mr Huey Long . . ." (F–B 436).[28] After the Southwestern graduation in early June the Tates returned to Benfolly, where Ford and Biala visited them in mid-June. Both guests were very tired from the long bus ride down from New York, Gordon told Katherine Anne Porter; the Master was "a little testy" and Janice "trying." But after all, it was "sweet of them to travel all that way down here to see us and we did have a good time. . . ."[29] But Ford could not for long stay away from his Provençal paradise, and by mid-July he and Janice were back at the Villa Paul.

The Tates settled in at Memphis for another year of teaching for Allen. Uninspiring as the Memphis milieu was, the job was a welcome means to pay off debts and stay clear of new financial worries. However, they had discovered another method to keep the specter of poverty off: to take part in conferences and short-term teaching engagements. Olivet College in Michigan offered one such welcome opportunity, beginning with the summer session in 1936. They encouraged Ford to join them for the July 1937 session.

During the year 1936 contacts between the two households were mostly carried on through sparse letters. The Tates were busy with teaching and writing and moving between Memphis, Benfolly, and Monteagle in Tennessee, where they stayed at the log cabin owned by their friend Andrew Lytle. Gordon took part in a drive to create a teaching position for Ford at Olivet College.[30] Ford was riddled with poor health, conflicts with publishers, and ever-increasing financial troubles. The hardest blow was no doubt the loss of the Villa Paul in the fall of 1936. In this sad situation, Biala felt that the Tates were "the only friends or family" they had, and Ford heartily agreed.[31] America still seemed to him his best bet for recognition and success. When he returned to New York at the end of November, the Tates were still staying at Monteagle. As before, he was ready to boost Gordon, and when her novel *None Shall Look Back,* dealing with the Civil War, appeared in early 1937, he offered glowing praise, comparing her work to that of Tolstoy and even the *Iliad* in that her novel was "most of all a landscape." She was for him "the most mysterious of writers": although as a person she was "vivid, brilliant, clamorous," her writings were characterized by "her calm self." Dealing with war and tragedy, her novel nevertheless had "a peculiar quality of tranquility."[32]

At the end of April the Tates left the safe harbor that Monteagle was to them—or at least to Gordon—and hastened home to Benfolly to make the house habitable after a two-year abandonment. Gordon was as ever one of Ford's most faithful friends, and the Tates graciously opened their house to him and his entourage, which consisted of Biala and her sister-in-law. The purpose was WORK. The guests arrived on May 14 and stayed till it was time for the Tates and Ford to go to Olivet for the July conference. There are several testimonies of these memorable weeks spent at Benfolly. Ford was as "difficult" as he could be; he was not well, suffering from insomnia, gout, and indigestion. Biala fought for his welfare, desiring nothing less than French cuisine, which Gordon and her cook adamantly refused to deliver: the fare was to be nothing but good southern cooking. Young Robert Lowell, putting up his tent on the Benfolly lawn, irritated Ford, whose mentorship the novice poet sought. The Tates liked "the Lowell boy," but Allen felt that he was "potentially a nuisance" (L–T 108). Lowell was hard to get rid of, though: he accompanied them to Olivet and from there to Boulder, Colorado, for another literary affair.

The Olivet connection proved useful to Ford. In his effort to make the college a cultural and educational force in the Midwest, the college president, Joseph Brewer, wished to secure his services as a lecturer and teacher. For Ford such an engagement was a way to obtain a stable source of income as well as to inculcate his ideas about civilization into the minds of a young American generation. An agreement was reached to the effect that he was to spend part of the year teaching at the college, in accordance with his own ideas and preferences. He would be able to share his time between America and France with Olivet as a fixed point. Accordingly, on March 23, 1938, he was on his way to the United States for a stint of teaching at Olivet. In early September he was still in Olivet, but planned to be in New York by mid-September (F–B 458).

The Tates had stuck it out at Southwestern for two years, and they were ready for a change of scene. Starting with the spring semester of 1938, they both held teaching positions at the Woman's College of the University of North Carolina at Greensboro (L–T 116). They spent the summer in West Cornwall, Connecticut, and after that breathing spell they were back in Greensboro. In April 1939 they took part in a writers' conference in Savannah, Georgia, where Gordon spoke on "The Southern Short Story" and "How a Short Story is Written." These were subjects where she could draw masterfully and pedagogically on her wide experience as a writer.

It turned out that she had a great gift for teaching about writing, and she spent a lot of time, care, and energy in advising young writers and students whom she believed in. At the invitation of the Tates, Ford, who was still in New York, came down to Greensboro in early March to speak to their students. His lecture to Gordon's class may have created certain difficulties, for his several health problems made for a wheezing, mumbling delivery, but, as Tate remembered, Ford "charmed and stimulated" his audience. Ford's profound fatigue may account for an outburst of displeasure with Gordon—the only one ever to be recorded, as far as I know: she had, against his will, arranged for a reception for him, and Ford revealed his resentment to Biala.[33] Even so, some time after this outburst of a man tired to the death, he evidenced his interest in Gordon the writer in a letter to Tate (*Letters* 319).

By this time Ford was in fact a dying man. As always he believed that France would benefit him and that French cuisine was the best remedy for his indigestion. At the end of May he therefore cut short his stay in America and sailed for Le Havre. We are familiar with the ending: how his condition worsened dramatically and how Normandy became his last resting place.

The Tates were spending the summer of 1939 at Monteagle near their friends the Andrew Lytles. One day in late June, Lytle's wife, Edna, showed Gordon a news story from Deauville in Normandy telling of Ford's death. Gordon immediately wrote to Biala: "I am too upset. We all are—we really can't quite take it in yet." But she was glad, she wrote, that he died in France, "for he loved it so" *(CG 42)*. Gordon, always a champion of Ford, at once took action to make Scribner's republish his best works. But it was to take a decade before even his masterpiece, the tetralogy, *Parade's End,* was republished as a unit (Knopf, 1950), with an introduction by Robie Macauley, once Ford's student at Olivet.[34]

Gordon kept up her contacts with Biala, sparse as they may have been. Biala brought remembrances of Ford; Gordon received a worn billfold. The Tates as usual moved from place to place, depending on where the job opportunities were. After three years of teaching at Princeton, Tate was offered a job in Washington, D.C., at the Library of Congress in 1943, and Biala saw them there. In the meantime she had married the artist Daniel Brustlein. Now it was Gordon's turn to paint a portrait of Biala. After a year in Washington, the Tates moved to Sewanee for Tate to take over the editorship of the *Sewanee Review* (L–T 204). Biala's picture of Good King René's castle at Tarascon found its place on the wall of their house to remind them of their days in the

Midi. Cap Brun, the Villa Paul, and the Villa les Hortensias offered
setting and atmosphere for a short story Gordon wrote at this time,
"The Olive Garden."

The Tates' marriage, from its very beginning a precarious relationship, broke down in 1945. Gordon was forced to leave Sewanee
by her husband, and she went to New York. She told her friends
Robert Lowell and his wife Jean Stafford that she could always be
reached through Janice Biala in New York. Later Biala found her a
place to live in the Village. It was a cold-water apartment at 108
Perry Street. The divorce took effect on January 8, 1946, but this
situation lasted only till April, when Gordon and Tate remarried.

Gordon had not forgotten Ford and his great influence on her
work and her views on writing. In her teaching at Columbia University, she referred to him as worthy of being studied by appren-
tice writers; she insisted on the rendering of the concrete detail
and on the importance of point of view, elements of technique that
Ford himself had excelled at.[35] In a commemorative issue of *New
Directions* (1942), she contributed a piece of homage, in which she
placed him in the company of the great Flaubert and Henry James.
She especially recommended that other novelists observe his mas-
terful handling of form.[36] When *Parade's End* was reissued in 1950,
she wrote a long review that appeared on the front page of the
New York Times Book Review. She focused on his "method," that is,
his Impressionist technique adopted by many later writers. Ford
was "the best craftsman of his day; we are only now beginning to
realize how widespread and pervasive such a literary influence can
be," she wrote. As for the tetralogy she praised Ford's skill as a
recorder of his time. She saw him as a brilliant historical novelist:
"At his touch some of history's driest, barest bones take on flesh."[37]
She alerted Biala to this review. To judge by a letter from Gordon
to Biala (at Princeton University Library), the latter wished for
stronger praise of Ford than Gordon offered.

In the early 1960s, after a second and final divorce from Allen Tate,
Gordon presumably felt a need to establish even more forcefully her
gratitude and loyalty to Ford the Master, and she published further
pieces praising him. In a brief homage, "To Ford Madox Ford," formed
as a letter addressed to him in the *Transatlantic Review,* she drew on
memories of their common "pursuit of good letters" and of his generosity to younger writers and his knack at recognizing talent.[38] Evidently editors and publishers regarded her as an expert on Ford, since
she had known him well and admired his work. In a special Ford Madox
Ford issue of the *Sewanee Review* in 1966, she contributed a substan-

tial article with the title "The Elephant." In this piece she commented on a number of books that dealt with Ford's oeuvre somewhat in the vein of blind men examining the various parts of the proverbial elephant. A convert to Catholicism, Gordon finds fault with these critics for being blind to the Roman Catholicism that, in her reading, "underlies all of Ford's fiction."[39] Her reverence and affection for Ford the Master color all her comments in a chapbook, *A Good Soldier: A Key to the Novels of Ford Madox Ford*, put out by the University of California Library in 1963. Here she takes up in greater breadth a point she had already made in her review of the *Parade's End* tetralogy: Ford's fascination with a *Belle Dame Sans Merci* character who appears in several of his novels, perhaps most prominently in the shape of Sylvia, Christopher Tietjens's merciless and bewitching wife. Gordon's main argument is that the key to his novels is precisely the drama created by his fictional hero's involvement with this temptress.[40]

Until the end Gordon cherished her memories of Ford and her friendship with him and his companions Stella Bowen and Janice Biala. She always kept the portraits that these two artists had painted of her and her family, and her favorite cookbook was *French Home Cooking* (Waldron 357), another tribute to Ford, who had always insisted on the superiority of *la cuisine française* for one's health and enjoyment.

Ford's significance for Gordon the writer was invaluable. He was one of the first to take a serious interest in her work; he prodded her into "fitting words together" regardless of inner and outer hindrances; and he offered both encouragement and constructive criticism. He set an example of the totally committed craftsman, working hard and with devotion, no matter where, when, or how. She needed this kind of model of patient and passionate discipline. Through him she learnt the importance of technique, lessons that she in turn transmitted to her students. She adopted some of the devices he mastered, such as the handling of timing and point of view, and perhaps also the rendering of local dialect (which *she* mastered in, for instance, the novel *Green Centuries*). Socially he was a great asset: she liked to be in his company, and when he was what some of his friends called "difficult," she seems to have had more patience with him than most.

For Ford the friendship between them also meant a great deal. Here was a talented, intelligent woman who, to some extent, depended upon his guidance for her development as a writer. Witty, aristocratically bohemian, she was good company, always willing to open her house to him. She was also concerned about doing her bit to further his opportunities in the United States. And, not least important, they shared a reverence for classical civilization and for a life informed by Mediterranean/southern values, such as conviviality and love of tradition and history. They both loved to care for things growing—flowers, vegetables, animals; their high regard for chickens as living creatures, for example, is colorfully reflected in the correspondence (above all in *CG 9* and *CG 10*).

To a reader with a deep and warm interest in the lives and works of both these writers, it adds a somewhat melancholy note to learn that among Gordon's papers there is a fragment with the title "A Fixed Abode."[41] For the two households—the Tates and the Fords—the fixed abode was surely the dream never to be realized. For Caroline Gordon home was a country house somewhere along the Kentucky–Tennessee border; for Ford Madox Ford it meant a villa, primitive if need be, but overlooking the fruitful country of Provence and the lovely Mediterranean Sea. Money determined to a great extent their limited chances of settling in their respective paradises, but certainly also—and perhaps in equal measure—their need to seek the stimulus of fellow artists and writers and ever new milieus. The cafés and restaurants of Paris had to be part of the scene, as well as New York with its opportunities for reaching an appreciative audience and finding a congenial brother- and sisterhood of art. But in whatever abode they were installed, these two artists devoted themselves, with dedication and passion, to the common art of fiction.

NOTES

1. The poet Christina Rossetti (1830–1894) was his aunt. Ford was christened Ford Hermann Hueffer; in 1919 he changed his name to Ford Madox Ford.

2. Arthur Mizener, *The Saddest Story: A Biography of Ford Madox Ford* (New York and Cleveland: The World Publishing Company, 1971), 352; hereafter referred to as Mizener within the text. In her article "Caroline Gordon, Ford Madox Ford: A Shared Passion for the Novel," *Southern Quarterly* 28 (3) (1990): 33–42, Deborah Core touches on certain aspects of the Gordon–Ford relationship, but she does not utilize their letters to each other.

3. *The Correspondence of Ford Madox Ford and Stella Bowen*, ed. Sondra J. Stang and Karen Cochran (Bloomington: Indiana Univ. Press, 1993), 207; hereafter abbreviated as F–B within the text.

4. Josephine Herbst, *The Starched Blue Sky of Spain and Other Memoirs* (New York: Harper Collins, 1991), 70.

5. See *Pound/Ford: The Story of a Literary Friendship*, ed. Brita Lindberg-Seyersted (New York: New Directions, 1982), 82; hereafter referred to as *Pound/Ford* within the text.

6. For example, by Ann Waldron in *Close Connections: Caroline Gordon and the Southern Renaissance* (Knoxville: Univ. of Tennessee Press, 1987), 56;

hereafter referred to as Waldron within the text. Cf. F–B 281 on the projected book.

7. Douglas Goldring, *South Lodge: Reminiscences of Violet Hunt, Ford Madox Ford and the English Review Circle* (London: Constable & Co., 1943), 179–80.

8. Calvin Fixx to Robert Cantwell, n.d., but late 1926 or early 1927. Univ. of Oregon Library. I thank Per Seyersted for calling my attention to this letter.

9. Quoted in W. J. Stuckey, *Caroline Gordon* (New York: Twayne, 1972), 13.

10. See Max Saunders, *Ford Madox Ford: A Dual Life,* vol. 2: *The After-War World* (New York: Oxford Univ. Press, 1996), 334–54; hereafter referred to as Saunders within the text.

11. Allen Tate, *Memoirs and Opinions, 1926–1974* (Chicago: Swallow Press, 1975), 54; hereafter referred to as *Memoirs* within the text.

12. Up to the end Elsie refused to agree to a divorce; she died in 1949.

13. Gordon to Josephine Herbst, Feb. 11, 1929. Yale Univ. Library.

14. *The Southern Mandarins: Letters of Caroline Gordon to Sally Wood, 1924–1937,* ed. Sally Wood (Baton Rouge: Louisiana State Univ. Press, 1984), 47; hereafter referred to as *Mandarins* within the text.

15. Veronica A. Makowsky, *Caroline Gordon: A Biography* (New York: Oxford Univ. Press, 1989), 87.

16. *FMF 2,* etc. = Ford's letter number 2, etc.; see the short chapter entitled "A Note on the Text" following.

17. Quoted in Gordon to Josephine Herbst, n.d., but fall of 1929. Yale Univ. Library.

18. Mentioned in Gordon to Josephine Herbst, n.d., but probably Jan. 1930. Yale Univ. Library.

19. *The Lytle–Tate Letters: The Correspondence of Andrew Lytle and Allen Tate,* ed. Thomas Daniel Young and Elizabeth Sarcone (Jackson: Univ. Press of Mississippi, 1987), 38; hereafter referred to as L–T within the text.

20. Ford Madox Ford, "A Stage in American Literature," *Bookman* 74 (Dec. 1931): 371–76.

21. James Maury Morris Gordon to Gordon, Jan. 13, 1932. Cornell Univ. Library. In the Cornell Univ. Library material, this letter is erroneously attributed to Janice Biala.

22. In the 1940s Janice Biala married the Alsace-born painter Daniel Brustlein (the Alain of the *New Yorker*) and moved to Paris, where she still lives and works.

23. Gordon to Léonie Adams, n.d., but probably fall of 1932. Yale Univ. Library reports that this letter, formerly among their holdings, is missing. Waldron quotes from it in *Close Connections,* 115.

24. Gordon to Katherine Anne Porter, [Sept. 1932]. Univ. of Maryland, College Park, Libraries.

25. Katherine Anne Porter to Peggy Cowley, Jan. 30, 1933. Univ. of Maryland, College Park, Libraries. (Possibly the draft of a letter that was never sent.)

26. "From Ford Madox Ford," reprinted in *Pound/Ford* 118.

27. *Letters of Ford Madox Ford,* ed. Richard M. Ludwig (Princeton: Princeton Univ. Press, 1965), 257; hereafter referred to as *Letters.*

28. For a report on the conference, see Thomas W. Cutrer, "Conference on Literature and Reading in the South and Southwest, 1935," *Southern Review,* n.s. 21 (Spring 1985): 260–300. See also Max Webb, "Ford Madox Ford and the Baton Rouge Writers' Conference," *Southern Review,* n.s. 10 (Autumn 1974): 892–903.

29. Gordon to Katherine Anne Porter, [June? 1935]. Univ. of Maryland, College Park, Libraries.

30. See Nancylee Novell Jonza, *The Underground Stream: The Life and Art of Caroline Gordon* (Athens: Univ. of Georgia Press, 1995), 174.

31. Ford to Allen Tate, Sept. 6, 1936 (*Letters* 257). It is only fair to note in connection with this statement that later in life, Biala expressed resentment of what she regarded as the Tates' duplicity; see Saunders 2: 656n. 25.

32. Ford Madox Ford, Scribner's in-house review in *Bookbuyer* for April 1937, 5–6. Princeton Univ. Library. This review is quoted from in Robert E. Golden and Mary C. Sullivan, *Flannery O'Connor and Caroline Gordon: A Reference Guide* (Boston: G. K. Hall, 1977), 216 (with the date given as March 1937).

33. Allen Tate quoted in Saunders 2: 541. Biala told Saunders about the incident (2: 540).

34. In this and the following two paragraphs, I rely on Waldron's *Close Connections* for certain factual details about contacts between Gordon and Biala after Ford's death.

35. See Danforth Ross, "Caroline Gordon's Golden Ball," *Critique* 1 (1) (Winter 1956): 67–73.

36. *New Directions*, Number Seven (Norfolk, Conn.: New Directions, 1942), 474–75.

37. Caroline Gordon, "The Story of Ford Madox Ford," *New York Times Book Review*, Sept. 17, 1950, 1, 22.

38. Caroline Gordon, "To Ford Madox Ford," *Transatlantic Review*, n.s. (1960): 5–6.

39. Caroline Gordon, "The Elephant," *Sewanee Review* 74 (4) (Autumn 1966): 856–71; quotation 863.

40. Caroline Gordon, *A Good Soldier: A Key to the Novels of Ford Madox Ford*, Chapbook No. 1 (Davis: Univ. of California Library, 1963).

41. In her biography (221) Makowsky quotes a passage from "A Fixed Abode."

A Note on the Text

A few types of emendations have been made in the printing of the letters: obvious spelling mistakes have been silently emended, as well as some other slips—for example, inconsistencies within a letter. Misspelled names have been left the way they were written, unless ambiguity has arisen. Certain idiosyncrasies have been retained, such as Ford's way of indicating the plural of names (e.g., "the Wright's"). His frequent ellipses have as a rule been kept within sentences and uniformly rendered by three dots, unless there seemed to be a special reason for other kinds; Gordon's rarer ellipses have either been transposed to three-dot signs or replaced by regular punctuation.

The following abbreviations are used: CG for Caroline Gordon; FMF for Ford Madox Ford; JB for Janice Biala; CUL for Cornell University Library; and PUL for Princeton University Library. Each letter is headed by initials and number, e.g., *FMF 1*. TLS stands for Typed Letter Signed and ALS for Autograph Letter Signed. The symbols l. and ll. indicate whether a letter consists of one or more leaves.

Characters figuring prominently in the correspondence include:

Allen: Allen Tate (1900–1974), poet and Gordon's husband.

Andrew: Andrew Lytle (1902–1995), writer and close friend of the Tates.

Gene: Eugene Pressly (1904–1979), employee in the U.S. foreign service and husband of Katherine Anne Porter. (In the correspondence, Pressly's name is sometimes misspelled "Pressleigh.")

Janice: Janice Biala (1903–), painter and Ford's companion in the 1930s.

Julie/Esther Julia: Julie (Esther Julia) Ford (1920–1985), Ford's daughter by Stella Bowen.

Katherine Anne/K.A.: Katherine Anne Porter (1890–1980), writer and friend.

Nancy: Nancy Tate Wood (1925–), daughter of the Tates.

Perkins: Maxwell Perkins (1884–1947), editor at Scribner's.

Red: Robert Penn Warren (1905–1989), poet, novelist, and friend of the Tates.

Sally: Sally Wood (1897–1985), close friend of Gordon.

Stella: Stella Bowen (1895–1947), painter and Ford's companion in the 1920s.

The Correspondence

❧

1930–1931

FMF 1. TLS. 1 l. Feb. 4, 1930. Paris.

4th Feb 1930

Dear Mrs Tate,

I am very glad you have decided to send your novel on its rounds. If an endorsement from me can do it any good, let me say that I have *never* in all the course of my literary experience had such a shock as that which attended my reading the first chapter of PENHALLY[1]—such a shock of real delight at the beauty of the writing and the handling of the material. That may have been partly because I have known you for a long time without your ever telling me that you wrote at all, but I am sufficiently hardened over reading first manuscripts to be pretty certain that surprise had little to do with the avidity with which I read the rest as far as it had gone. I won't say that I have never read anything in [the] way of first novels that I liked as well but I am certain that I never did read one that I liked better. That being so I am quite confident that if it is at all properly published it will have at least quite a respectable sale and, the tide setting at the moment behind that sort of book there is no reason why the sale should not be quite a very large one. As to that I am ready to pledge my critical reputation, such as it is. And moreover I am quite certain that in a very few years' time your name will be one to do honour to any publisher's list.

Please, if you think it will be useful, shew this letter to any publisher whom you choose to select.

Believe me

Always very sincerely yours
Ford Madox Ford

1. See introduction, XVIII–XIX.

FMF 2. TL (incomplete). 1 l. Feb. 24, 1930. Paris.

24th Feb 1930

Dear, dear Caroline,

I have had three letters and the ms from you all together.[1] It is lovely to have them but dreadful to think that they are such a long time in coming and the letters of mine that they answer were sent so long ago. One of yours is dated Jan 8th but I think it must be Feb 8th and I hope so because it is the nicest—and it is nicest to have the last the nicest.

I will answer them in the order they seem to be written in.

Yes, I know you must be in a desperate state over your novel but you *must* finish it. The fragment you have sent me is lovely—but I will write about that at the end—and indeed I know what you mean when you say you feel like half a person but you cannot wish you could see me half as much as I wish I could see you. I don't, heaven knows, *want* you to read my earlier books for they are dreadful stuff, but I think you are mistaken in being afraid of influences. They are things one must go through to be a complete person—I mean that they are like the measles, things one must go through or one is always in danger of catching them and they affect one worse the later one takes them. Besides you have much too strong an individuality ever to be swamped by me. It is only in just the telling of the story—the skeleton—that I can influence you and that is purely a mechanical matter. I mean that is outside the art and personality of the writer which are the valuable things.

Dear, your letters are not unsatisfactory. How could you imagine that I could mean anything of the sort? They are you and I want nothing better.

I do not see how I shall get to the U.S. before the Fall. It is really a matter of money and that largely depends on what happens to my books which, at present are in a most hopeless tangle—mostly because of Macaulay's. If you see Susie[2] you might tell her that I will answer her letter—received today—as soon as I have had time to think about it. The point is that Firman[3] has delayed things for so long that he has lost me the Spring season for NOTTERDAM[4] and that is really atrocious because it practically means I lose a whole year. As it is I imagine what I shall have to do will be to drop NOTTERDAM for several years and concentrate on getting the HISTORY[5] published by the fall, coming over then. You see I can hang on here without American publication but I can't afford to live in N.Y. without it and Firman is so unreasonably dilatory that I do not think that I can contemplate continuing with him. He had NOTTERDAM over four months before I told Ruth Kerr[6] to take it away from him and I certainly do not mean to let him have the ms again unless he likes to make a definite offer of it. You might adumbrate the above to Susie if you liked to because I cannot very well write her an official letter to that effect—but there is no need for its being adumbrated and you may just as well keep out of my affairs, if you feel like it.

But, dear, you may be quite certain that whenever I do strike the United States I shall come quite straight to you, even if it were only to be turned down when I got to you. But you seem to want me to come and I can't say what life that gives me.

I certainly shall be glad when you are out of N.Y., though I suppose that means that you will be further away and letters will take a long time to reach you as if it didn't take long enough already. Still I am sure you will be the better for it. And certainly I will stay a long time—perhaps for ever, for I have practically nothing to bring me back here.

My life here is perfectly tranquil. I stop indoors all day and see no-one at all except the Trasks[7] who are ever faithful. I have given up the sonnet parties[8] because they bored me when you were no longer there. I go in the evenings to the Deux Magots and read the INTRANSIGEANT and as there is no-one there that I know I speak to no-one.

The poor Trasks are in great tribulation because that fellow, Williams has not sent her over a copy of the divorce—or rather has only sent an uncertified photographic copy which is no good, and so they can't get married and it will take who knows how long to get a properly certified copy. They are really very miserable because the delay is rather disastrous. Don't however mention this because I believe they plan to say very shortly that they *are* married.

Good for the ground hog: it has been pretty fine here but I have been rather crippled by sciatica for the last fortnight, however I suppose that will go when the fine weather sets in.

Estill Springs [Tenn.] certainly sounds fascinating. I don't see why I should take a dislike to your father though I don't see why he shouldn't take a dislike to me. Still that's rather meeting trouble. I can generally make people like me if I want to. I am a little regretful that you are not going to your birthplace[9] because I should love the place where you were born wherever it is—but then I shall love better any place where you were so it is all one where you go. I live for nothing but the time when I shall see you next.

Do you understand what it is? Nothing has any colour; nothing has any interest. It is all one long drag of days like being in a [The rest of the letter is missing.]

1. These letters are missing. Gordon sent part of *Penhally* for Ford to comment on.
2. Susan Jenkins Brown, adviser to the Macaulay Company.
3. Or Furman? cf. *FMF 4*; associated with the Macaulay Company.
4. The story about Joseph Notterdam became the novel *When the Wicked Man* (1931).
5. *A History of Our Own Times*, published posthumously by the Indiana State University Press (1988) and in England by Carcanet (1989).
6. Ford's literary agent in New York.
7. Willard Trask, translator, and his future wife, Mary McIntosh, a dancer, shared Ford's household in Paris for a brief period of time in 1930.
8. See introduction, xvi.
9. Gordon was born in Kentucky at a place near the Tennessee border.

FMF 3. ALS. 1 l. Mar. 25, 1930. Paris.

25 March 1930

My dear, dear Caroline:

I have your letter[1] of the 11th but though you can't believe how it pleases me to have it you can't also believe how it perturbs me because the address is only Merry Mont (no State) & the postmark is Trenton—but also no state. Now Trenton I am almost certain is Ky whilst I almost certainly remember to have heard you say that you were born just across the border in Va. So to where am I to write to you? Will you ever get this.

And then: you know my *whole* life & plans in every thing depend on seeing you & soon. I can't go on much longer without it. I have kept that *motif* out of my letters because I did not want to harass you. But—if you are going to "build a house at Little West Fork"[2]—will there be any pub. or boarding house near there where I cd. stay?

You see I had made up my mind to emigrate to the U.S.A. for good when I leave here this time: but if I can't get near you, what is the good? If you *could* cable me an answer to this it wd. help me so very much. Just cable "Yes" & your correct postal address for next month *with State*, if there wd be any chance of my finding shelter near Little West Fork—& if you want me to come.

It is very late & I am very tired: this is like the letters I write you every night & don't mail. One day you will see them all! Oh my dear: it gets worse & worse. I can't go on. This is to catch the majestic tomorrow.

Yr. own
F

I am so glad of all your Scribner news.[3]

1. This letter is missing.
2. The Little West Fork of the Red River was one of the places Gordon and her husband considered as suitable for a prospective home for themselves (Waldron 80).
3. Gordon had been offered an advance on *Penhally* to be published by Scribner's, as well as for a short story to appear in *Scribner's* magazine (Waldron 80).

FMF 4. TLS. 3 ll. Apr. 2, 1930. Paris.

2 April 1930

Dear, Dear Caroline,

I have just received your letter of the 14th March[1]—and as it answers mine of the 24th February, see how long it takes to get any answer. However, now I know in what State you at least temporarily are, you may hear from me a little more quickly, though I suppose speed does not in the long run make very much difference. Or perhaps it does since one wants to think of a person as he or she is at the moment and conditions change so rapidly. I mean it pleases me to think of you fairly prosperous and confident among jonquils and plum blossoms and old houses that fall down quietly, but I suppose that whilst I am writing this the jonquils and plum blossoms are over and your new house is going up[2]—I hope gaily and noisily. And perhaps too you have written a great deal more in your novel [*Penhally*]. But anyhow your conditions must be a great deal more congenial to you than almost any in which I have known you—except, say . . . or I should like to think it, having tea Chez Fast with the taxis running below in the rue Royale.

My dear, I don't suppose we shall ever meet again—at least I have been feeling a strong conviction to that effect for the last few days. But I go on making plans—to take a French boat to New Orleans and then go up the river, say as far as Cairo, and then strike across in your direction and settle down near you . . . till death us do part. But I daresay that is the last thing you might wish and I see no chance of my being able to do it for years—and I shan't last for years. My "circumstances" are very bad and grow steadily worse. This book[3] goes on getting longer and longer and, even though I may see the end of it, it is not yet sold and even when it is there will be no money to it, so at best I can do no more than dig myself in here and go on living like an eremite.

I daresay Ruth Kerr is dilatory, as you suggest, but not more dilatory than anyone else; but as for Macaulay and NOTTERDAM I told her myself specifically and formally to get that ms away from Furman and not to let them have it again. They had already had it for nearly six months and I knew they did not want to publish it—which is what Miss [Susan] Jenkins tells me in her last letter. Furman, I mean, kept on letting me know that he would settle about it as soon as he could get hold of Guinsberg[4] but he never did get hold of Guinsberg and if he could not do that in six months his eagerness could not have been sufficient to make me want to be published by him.

It is repulsive writing this sort of thing to you but it—this sort of thing or something like it—is always at the bottom of the Life Literary and I have grown to view it with complacency or at any rate without much agitation. You write a book without any arrière pensée and then for some reason that would appear quite esoteric from the aesthetic point of view one Jew, or two, or six, is determined that the book shall not be published. I guess Mr Furman and Mr Guinsberg are if not in open, then in tacit, cahoots to prevent the book being published by one another or by anyone else probably because it tells too much about what publishing really is.[5] That never occurred to me whilst I was writing it and it would not have made any difference to me if it had. And I don't really much care; the book can wait. What really interests me is that it should get published one day and that Julie should get some money out of it.

Otherwise I am steeped to the heart in the eighties and nineties[6] and the world of today hardly exists for me—except for you, shadowy and so extraordinarily real, walking about ruined choirs amongst daffodils that are by now as dead as the eighties. It is a queer muddle or it would be if there were any Purpose. One is so used to think of the miracles of Scientific thought that have conquered space and time and all the rest of it that it seems to be only a bad joke on the part of the Provvi that I can't just walk out into the Luxemburg and see you beside the statue of Verlaine that is in Kentucky. And one has only minutes to live and all this time is being wasted. I seem to be gradually dying from the feet upwards, at any rate I go out so little that when I do go out I can hardly walk and I have aged so visibly in the last three months that I could not bear to have you see me. So it's just as well that we shan't meet again. In any case, in a very short time all that will remain of me will be just in your memory and I'd just as lief you did not remember me as half moribund. I suppose though, it does not matter much as long as it's one's brain that dies last.

I enclose a picture of Cooper's, Bedham, Fittleworth, Sussex—where

Julie was born, or where she would have been born if that had not taken place in a nursing home. I don't suppose your house will be much like it but I hope Nancy will enjoy running about it as much as Julie used to do in the other place. All the grass you see in the picture will at this moment be invisible for daffodils running right up the bank; the big box hedge in the middle distance was said to be four hundred years old and so was the house except that I built the porch and the window above it. Old Cooper, the tenant who died when I took it over, was 82 and his father before him 85 yet the only window in the bedroom which I replaced was not as large as a pocket-handkerchief and did not open. Tempi passati . . . tempi passati . . .

I wonder often how you are getting on with your novel; I think what makes me most impatient of all is not being able to look over your shoulder while you write. I think I could make it much easier for you.

I don't think I have any news. Helen Cros[7]—so the Bandys[8] say—has lost her job at the American Library, I don't know why, and slapped the face of Dr Stevenson, I equally don't know why, but I don't know what she is doing instead. The [Willard and Mary] Trasks are to be married in London tomorrow. I don't know when they are coming back. The Boydens[9] having returned from Prague on Monday are setting out for the Riviera this evening. I went to a party at the Bandys last night and we played anagrams. At the Deux Magots the night before we played auction—Baker,[10] Alice Bandy, Bird[11] and myself. I *have* known worse players than Baker but I can't remember who they were. So, as I played with him all the evening I lost twenty francs. I also lost my cigarette case which grieves me. On the other hand Baker is writing a novel which is *very* beautiful in spots. He's really rather a remarkable young man. A girl is coming from California, with mother complete, to marry him here in June.

Does your father play auction? If so, when I come I may lose some more. Oh, my dear if I only could.

I wonder if you understand at all how it is with me? In the little letters I write you every night and that you will get one day you might discover. But you probably won't.

Goodbye, my dear. Think of me sometimes, but think more about your work. I am so pleased when I think that that is going on.

Your own

F

1. This letter is missing.

2. By mid-March the Tates were making arrangements to move to what became their house Benfolly, situated in the Cumberland Valley, Tennessee; they were still staying at Merry Mont, Gordon's grandmother's place across the border in Kentucky.

3. Presumably *A History of Our Own Times*.

4. Harold Guinzberg of the Viking Press.

5. *When the Wicked Man* displays an American publishing world full of corruption and cynicism.

6. Referring to the book of reminiscences *Return to Yesterday* (1931).

7. Probably Helen Crowe, a friend of Katherine Anne Porter and radical journalist Dorothy Day from Greenwich Village.

8. William O. Bandy was a classmate of Allen Tate's, later professor of French; wife Alice.

9. Polly Chase Boyden and her husband, wealthy people from Chicago.

10. Howard Baker, a novelist and poet from California, had had a hand in the starting of the magazine *Gyroscope*, which published Gordon's story "Summer Dust" in the fall of 1929. His wife Dorothy wrote the novel *Young Man with a Horn* (1938), inspired by the jazz music of Bix Beiderbecke (1901–1931).

11. William Bird, publisher of the Three Mountains Press in Paris; a friend of Ford's since *transatlantic review* days.

CG 1. TLS. 1 l. [Sept. 1930] [Benfolly]

Dearest Ford:

I am so glad to know that you are in New York, though I had you pictured as sitting happily in the sunshine at the Deux Magots for another month or two yet. Anyhow, it's grand to know that you are here. You must come down here before the cold weather sets in. It is grand now. I've been trying all morning to work, but it's hard. There is so much activity going on outside. Mr. Perry's[1] two mules dash over the lawn, dragging wagon loads of dirt. They are followed by our colored henchman, Jim [Hughes], Allen, Nancy, Freda, the shepherd dog and all the chickens. There is a great deal of shrieking and shouting and clucking. They are making a circular drive and gravelling it and God knows what else. It is all going to be very grand, though, when they get through.

We have had company, company, company all summer. But it's all over, thank God. I have lots written on my novel [*Penhally*] that I'm dying to show you.

I wrote one of the Nashville club ladies about getting a lecture for you there. Unfortunately, though, I didn't start in time—I never realized that the creatures get these things up months ahead. She says they have spent all their money, but they are trying to get some more up. This one, a friend of ours, who is managing things, will make them dig up the money if there is any to dig. She is awfully anxious for you to come.

The Cowleys, Malcolm and Peggy, by the way, are driving down here around October third. Can't you get a ride with them? The Slater Browns[2] say they are coming Thanksgiving—if you don't fancy driving a thousand miles or so with Peggy! (Malcolm is at the New Republic now.)

Nancy was much cut up yesterday because we wouldn't allow her to attend the funeral of her great-great-great uncle. She said "I went to a funeral every day in Paris, with Madame Gau."[3] And I'll bet she did. She said the other day "I reckon Estair Julia is a grown lady now."

Red Warren arrived from England the other day and we all drank beer and sat in the sun and then went in swimming and sat in the sun and drank some more beer. There is really no news from us. That's the way the summer has gone, except that we have a cook who gets us up with the dawn, so we get quantities of work done before the day has even started.

I'm so glad you're on this side of the water,

As always,

C.

1. A tenant.
2. William (Bill) Brown, novelist, and his wife Susan (Sue) Jenkins Brown.
3. Nancy's nanny during the Tates' stay in Paris in 1928–29.

FMF 5. TLS. 3 ll. Sept. 25, 1931. Toulon.

25 Sept 1931

Dearest Caroline,

It is truly a scandal that I have not written to you for so long—and the only excuse, that material circumstances have been almost too heavy for me is not much of an excuse. I don't even know that I have ever told you that we had settled in here.[1] We did that on the first of March. We have a terrace looking onto the Mediterranean and a number of terraces of garden below. We have finished our sweet corn and water melons but still have tomatoes, chilis, eggplants and most of the lesser vegetables which will begin to flourish now that the winter approaches. We had a considerable drought all through the spring and summer—no rain at all from the beginning of March till the end of August, though that is normal, after that some fierce storms that washed half the things out of the ground. One drowned seventeen men in the sea under our eyes—though that too is normal, the Mediterranean being a treach-

erous syren. We ourselves did not have more than three days of
extreme heat up here, but down in the town it was sometimes pretty
terrible—and even down on our lower terraces. The sirocco, when
it blows—it being Norman Douglas' South Wind[2]—is as bad as
its reputation. It saps all your vitality. You lie about cursing the
world and quarrelling with every one near you and meditating deeds
of unimaginable blackness. Then with the mistral in the evening,
quite suddenly, you are all sweetness and light. The mistral is a
terrific north wind that destroys everything it meets and drives the
sea to agony but it is called the Health of Provence and is indeed
that. Fortunately you do not have the sirocco for more than two or
three days in the summer.

I tell you all this, not so much to be topographical as—as no
doubt you guess, to try to trepan you into coming here, as well as
to pose us in your mind. In those surroundings we have gardened,
cooked, washed. painted, written and lived. We see hardly anybody except French people—the only Transatlantic exceptions having been a young fellow called George Davis who has written rather
a good book called THE OPENING OF A DOOR,[3] some unknowns from
Cagnes, Peggy Guggenheimer[4] and her young man, and a Miss
Loeb who is no relation of Harold.[5] Of French we see a few painters, writers and titled people who are decorous and amiable but
very dull—all of them, painters and writers included. Oh, and of
course the Hersch's.[6] Virginia will pass but a lot of Lee is like having had a surfeit of blotting paper. Their main conversation centred
round the matrimonial misfortunes of George Seldes[7] who having
carried off Nathan Ash's[8] countess proceeded to make lurid the
neighbouring village of Bandol by his carryings on when the young
lady alternately left him and returned.

The Town indeed, like the Heathen, doth furiously rage with
Montparnassians beneath our feet whilst we high-hat them. We have
had the most exciting news from young George Davis. They come
down in big drunk drafts, abide their stated time, fight, attempt suicide, enlist in the Foreign Legion and go away. One B.D.D. consist-
ing of people whom we mostly all know had for its stated time six
days and was then run out. But, as the autumn falls, quiet returns. We
have our own private feud. Mr W. Seabrook[9] who now signs himself
"Seabrook" tout court, like an English peer persuaded my landlady to
let him my cherished studio in the port, over my head. That is why we
had to take this place. So we walk the streets of Toulon and so does
William and we look right through him. He on the other hand walks
among the dock hangers on like a modest ballon saying: "Je suis ung

aicrivaing. J'aycrie des livers. Sayt ung métier comm ung auter." As who should say: "I am a writer. I write books. It is a trade like another." The crowd exclaims reverentially "Quel homme vertueux que Monsieur Seeahbroo! Comme il est modeste!," modesty and virtue being his note amongst all the other scandals of the sea-port. He acquired these attributes in Ethiopia. How truly he wrote who first said: "Semper aliquid novi ex Africa!"[10]

Janice has acquired fluent French, beats down the marketwomen's prices like the most accomplished of French housewives, paints a great deal, says she will never paint again, paints some more, has acquired a permanent wave and is contemplating as the days draw in, acquiring a goat skin coat. As you did not previously know Janice these items will not startle you so much as they will, say, Provincetown.

As for me, I have lost a great deal of flesh, written a book,[11] published another,[12] am contemplating another,[13] have produced an infinite number of vegetables, had some chickens and ducks stolen, cook really remarkable meals, go about extravagantly ragged except on the rare occasions when I take Julie to Mass. Julie has just gone back to Paris for the rentrée de classe.[14] She has been down here nearly ten weeks. We purpose—if Liveright sends us any money, though that is not his strong suit—going up to Paris for the winter, about the end of November and not returning here till March in order to re-start the garden which will sleep well till then. Couldn't you manage to spend the winter in Paris—or part of it in Paris and part in this place? The house is not wildly convenient but you could just get into it—I mean, you, Allen and Nancy—and living is very cheap if you at all know the ropes and not extravagantly dear even if you don't. Do think of it. Nothing could give me greater pleasure and I am sure it would be a success. I am of course hoping that PENHALLY will do that great conjuring trick.

I have kept, naturally, speaking of that until I had got rid of the above trivialities. It arrived just four days ago and had for me all the aspects of a fairy tale come true. I have for so long been used to thinking of you working at PENHALLY that the aspect of the book and the thought that you *weren't* any more worrying over it seemed almost unreal.

I have not yet had time really to get hold of it as much as I eventually shall—after having read it once or twice again but I have got hold of it enough to see that it does immensely come off. All the earlier part is almost without equal and the later chapters are at least without anything that is superior in the best—the very best

American writing. That, in spite of your weaving the subject back-
wards and forwards, which was the only way to treat it, the book
breaks back when you come to the moderner parts was inevitable.
On such an immense canvas the subject is bound to grow too strong
for one—or rather, for the atmosphere of the work as a whole. I
think you might have got a little more unity by emphasising the
physical aspects of Penhally itself in the later chapters. It is very
right to let the characters remember continually what stood here
or there at such and such a time but it might have been as well if
you had written yourself directly what changes, at given moments,
had occurred here and there. Of course I recognise you doing it, in
the clearing away of cottages and trees under Mrs Parrish and the
consequent change in the view.

And I can't—you can't expect me to!—like the dénouement. That
is only my aggravating way and, if as I suspect, it was Mr Perkins
who pressed you to "end" the book only Mr Perkins will be aggra-
vated—which I hope he will be good and strong.

But when all that is said it remains a wonderful book—quite as
wonderful as I expected it to turn out—and that was no little thing.
If it does not quite completely, absolutely and to the last drop, come
off that is because the subject is so vast that you would have had to
take ten years to it—and no doubt it is better that you should get
on to other things. I won't write any more about it now because I
intend, when I have read it again to write a review of it which I
will send to Perkins on the chance of his finding someone to print
it. If he does not, get him to send it to you unprinted. I could say a
great deal more to you now—but as the unknown lady said to Maria:
"Praise to the face is open disgrace."

The chief cause for dissatisfaction for me is that the book is *not*
dedicated to me. It would have been my chief claim to fame and
my greatest literary pleasure if it had been. I can't think how you
could have imagined that I would have refused. As far as I can
remember it was you who refused to let *me* dedicate a book to you.
But the next thing to go on to is the arranging how we are to meet
again and how we shall work again at things. It will have to be you
that come over here for I see no chance of our ever getting to Tennessee—or indeed ever anywhere. What I—and that of course includes Janice—want is that you should stay for a time with us and
then occupy whichever of our houses we aren't occupying—which
could be whichever you chose. As we scheme it now this place will
be vacant from November to March and 32 [rue de Vaugirard] from

March to July when my lease expires and the house is to be torn down. So make up a plan and let us know quickly, quickly!

All sorts of good wishes for the little family

Yr

Ford M.F.

of course it's a swell book!

Dear Caroline

Ford, as usual, is too critical. I think your book is swell all over & the last part endears itself to me by its fine slang. I haven't heard any for a long time & it makes me feel good. One should always consider the poor exiles I think, among the haw-hawing English. Of course if *I'd* made the slightest criticism he'd have socked me. Please do come.

Janice

1. The Villa Paul at Cap Brun, Toulon.
2. English novelist, author of *South Wind* (1917).
3. *The Opening of a Door* was published in London in 1931.
4. Peggy Guggenheim, wealthy American art collector, who lived in Paris in the 1930s; after World War II she established herself in a Venetian Palazzo, which became an informal art museum.
5. Harold Loeb, the "model" for Hemingway's character Robert Cohn in *The Sun Also Rises.*
6. Lee Hersch, painter, and Virginia Hersch, novelist.
7. American reporter and foreign correspondent.
8. Nathan Asch, Polish-born American novelist.
9. William (Willie) Seabrook, author of *Jungle Ways* (1931); he occupied Stella Bowen's studio in Toulon.
10. "Always something new from Africa!"
11. *Return to Yesterday,* published November 2, 1931.
12. *When the Wicked Man,* May 20, 1931.
13. Probably *The Rash Act* (1933).
14. "Back-to-school."

CG 2. TLS. 3 ll. [Oct. 1931] [Benfolly]

My dearest Ford:

I see now that it was indescribably stupid in me not to know that it would please you to have "Penhally" dedicated to you. God knows I would have if it had occurred to me that it would give you even a moment's pleasure. You *are* vain—I ought to have seen that the gesture might please you. But really I think of you as being vain about more frivolous things—cooking?—I *knew* all along that you would be disappointed in the book—it seemed silly to dedicate it to you. It is impossible, though, to forgive people for being stupid—I know that. I can only remind you that living so long on the edge of things as I have, I have cast aside a great many amenities that some people manage to hang on to. I just have these blind spots. Sometimes I come up against them and feel rather silly as I do now. The other day, for instance, some old fool wanted a picture of Allen to include in her "Famous Clarksvillians." There was a horrible picture of Allen that I really wanted to get out of the house. I was on the point of mailing it to her when Allen said reproachfully that he didn't want people to think he looked like that. Honestly, it had never occurred to me that he would give a damn what the Clarksville people thought he looked like.

As a matter of fact it had never entered my head not to dedicate "Penhally" to you until last fall when you were here. You did tell me not to when I mentioned it; I see now it was a perfunctory remark, but I am so used to accepting your judgment about things that what you said stuck in my mind, though I never seemed to have the chance afterwards to ask you why you said that. I should have found time, of course. Honestly, it never occurred to me that I had anything worth while to lay at your feet. In conversation, all the time, with other writing people, and God knows I see too many of them, I try to put into words what you have done for me, simply because it is an amazing thing and to me an exciting topic of conversation—if I should ever amount to anything everybody will know that it is your doing—but it is, really, I know, that you have a special fondness for this book over which you worked so hard and another, better book of mine might be dedicated to you and give you no pleasure . . . Hell! But there's no use talking about it.

As for "Penhally" itself, the less said the better, I suppose. It was, as you say, too big an undertaking. The hell of it is that I feel I'd have been equal to it if I'd had the time. It would have taken at least another year, maybe more. I was terribly harried towards the last, by my family, by Perkins—I worked under tremendous difficulties. My aunt,[1] who several years ago, nursed me through a nervous collapse of two months during which I lay in bed unable to walk, fell ill herself and had to cast on me a Confederate veteran who has very set ideas on woman's place in a home.

The denoument is not in any way to be blamed (?) on Perkins. He is rather puzzled by it and has had to convince himself several times that it is right. It is, you know, implicit in the plot from the beginning. I wrote another ending in which the young man went out on the porch and looked around and the land which he had known seemed to have been obliterated—I believe the last words were "as if by a wave of the hand." Thinking about it I became convinced that reflection wouldn't do, that there must be some symbol of the destruction of the house and only violent action would suffice for that. I may have been influenced by Allen; he thought that too. With me, towards the last, it was a question of whether to end the thing in Chance's consciousness or with the picture of him moving in this changed world—melodrama, I know, that last sentence about calling the sheriff. I read the whole book over three or four times and each time it built up to that last gesture.

I wish I could have laid the book aside for a month or two, but Perkins was writing for it all the time and my uncle[2] who had unfortunately just recalled that it took Gray seven years to write "The Elegy in A Country Churchyard" was calling me up every morning to know if I wasn't through by this time. A curious thing, and this, really, is responsible for the denoument, dislike it as you may— several years ago I wrote a novel which was really a section of this present book and it ended with one brother shooting another. Allen says I have a bad homicidal complex.

But enough of all this. It was so good to hear from you again and as you say to be able to pose you all in our minds. I have not known where you were. I am so delighted that you have established a menage where you can be in the sun and can lie about cursing the world in general, instead of particular people as one does so much in cities. We guffawed heartily over [William] Seabrook and Africa. It really is shameful about that studio. Allen says that after all he would rather live among the Meriwethers than the Montparnassians—that the Meriwethers take only time from you. To think that when you were here I never even took you to Meriville! You might have enjoyed seeing the old graveyard and would surely have enjoyed commenting on how new it looked. We did one thing when somebody, I forget who was here, that we should have done when you were here. We started out one day after lunch and drove all around the Meriwether block of land, getting home at seven o'clock. We saluted such of the kin as we met along the way with a new respect, marvelling how those dull and loutish people had managed to stay put with when most of us are so hurled about the world. Oh, it was Mark Van Doren,[3] whose people are Illinois farmers; we would show him what we considered level stretches and he would say, "Oh, but that is almost a mountain."

I have been reprimanded severely by Cousin Gus Henry, by the way, for having a blasted sycamore in my book. "Don't you know that lightning never strikes a sycamore tree?" he says. But Mr. Gus

Williams, of Peacher's Mill, has come to my rescue, saying that he in his lifetime has known three sycamores to be struck.

I am going to apply for a Guggenheim again, just to be doing it. I don't imagine there's any chance. And I fear "Penhally" will never send me abroad. I have no idea how it is selling or being reviewed, for that matter. A letter from John Peale Bishop[4] this morning said that Perkins was the most depressed man he'd seen out of banking circles. And the letters Perkins writes me are certainly fraught with gloom. I do wish we *could* get over. We could arrange about this place all right. Some of these numerous cousins might be induced to take it over for a year. Allen has never finished Lee,[5] but he has an idea for another book as soon as he does get it off his hands. I got an advance, only five hundred, on a second novel,[6] but it went like the wind.

I wish you had told me what sort of book you are contemplating now.

I wish I could see Janice's portrait of you. It looks good. The snapshots are charming. Allen says he likes Janice's looks so much.

Allen and I are going the last of this week to Charlottesville, Virginia, to attend "the Southern Writers' Conference." It ought to be a very amusing affair, Cabell[7] and Glasgow[8] and all the galvanized Yankees. Old Marse Phelps Putnam,[9] as he calls himself, says he is coming, though uninvited, being from Boston. I shall insist on his using his Southern accent that he acquired on this front porch while he is there. We don't exactly know how we will get there, having no money, but I suppose we'll manage it. Allen has an arrangement now to do one article a month for the New Republic, which helps some.

Malcolm and Peggy Cowley have separated. Peggy is in Mexico and Malcolm is running the New Republic. I don't really know any other gossip. Katherine Anne Porter, after promising to come by here, counted up her money and rushed off to Europe on a Norddeutscher Lloyd boat which took her to Germany,[10] though she had had no intention of going to Germany. I hope you all see her if you go to Paris this winter. If you do see her, enjoy her society but don't try to do anything about her. She is one of the finest writers now living and she will kill herself very soon, by living in the wrong climate or wasting herself on idiotic people or anything else that is suicidal enough. But there is nothing anybody can do about it. The trip abroad is perfectly characteristic. She would start off for France and land in Germany, and then stay there in the cold all winter.

We have our farm really a little in hand for next year, I think. Our next door neighbor[11] is going to take it over. He is perfectly honest and a very hard worker so we may expect a little revenue from it. And for odd job man we have Mr. Norman[12] living in the cabin in the woods. He is "sanctified" and boasts that nobody has ever heard him swear. Allen says he hopes Mr. N. will never hear me swear or he'll certainly quit us.

I am writing a long story (20,000 words) which I'm going to enter in Scribner's long story contest, hoping not to win the prize but that they'll buy the story as they do many of those entered. It is called "To Cumberland."[13] (You say "Cumber *Land*.") I am having a great time, reading about pioneer times. Not being here you will be spared a lot. Allen has had to hear all about Jenny Wiley and Dr. Thomas Walker and the Harp brothers until he is pretty worn out. One advantage you have in writing about those times— you start off in an atmosphere of tremendous excitement. The exploits of some of those pioneer women are things that occur usually only on battlefields.

Red and Cinina Warren are going to be in Nashville this winter, Red taking John Ransom's[14] place at Vanderbilt. They make a fine addition to our small social circle, though Cinina is very trying. She has been threatened with tb and has to be very careful of her health and all the time one wonders why this futile, noisy life has to be preserved at the expense of Red who really is quite a person, and such a talented writer.

Please thank Janice heartily for her kind words about "Penhally." I am glad she liked it. I am glad, too, that you think it as good as you do; as I say I knew that you would be a little disappointed, and that made me feel pretty bad. For weeks after I finished it I couldn't bear to think of it and it is only in the last week that I have had any mind at all to write again. Now at any rate in the immortal words of Roberta[15] "something is transpiring within me" and I am certainly going to work like hell this winter. I have really been afraid to work until just recently, I was so tired.

The novel I am working on now is about two families, white and poor white, living on the same land. It is hard to understand poor white people—I know that it is praiseworthy to write about them! There are so many things that have to be comprehended and yet are hard to put into such a novel—the terrible and swift deterioration of a whole people after the Civil war—you see it in architecture, my grandmother and her husband deserting a really beautiful house like the Old Place to live in an atrocity like the

Merry Mont house—But it pervades the whole fabric of society—
my grandmother says of two cousins who turned Republican that
"they grew up after the Civil war when people had no principles."

I have to go now to take one of the Dominican Sisters out for a
drive. This sister and a little girl, who seems to be called "Okra,
junior" now dominate our whole lives. Everything has to be to their
taste. Nancy has just come in, wearing a long dress of mine and
with her cheeks highly rouged. She sends love to Julie—but Julie
is back in Paris by this time.

Love to you and Janice,

as ever,

C.

1. Margaret (Pidie) Meriwether Campbell.
2. Robert Emmet Meriwether.
3. Novelist, poet, and professor at Columbia University.
4. Poet and novelist.
5. Allen Tate's biography of Robert E. Lee, never completed.
6. *A Morning's Favour,* later retitled *The Garden of Adonis* (1937).
7. James Branch Cabell, prolific novelist, poet, and critic; best known for
   his pseudo-learned historical romances.
8. Ellen Glasgow, author of a series of novels set in Virginia from 1850 to
   the 1940s.
9. A Yale graduate, whose verse Allen Tate admired; Putnam and his wife,
   Una, became close friends of the Tates.
10. It was on this voyage that Katherine Anne Porter found the material for
    what became her best-selling novel *Ship of Fools* (1962).
11. A German tobacconist.
12. A tenant.
13. Later retitled "The Captive."
14. John Crowe Ransom, influential Tennessee poet and leader of the group
    of Agrarians, who advocated an agrarian economy for the South.
15. A cook.

CG 3. TLS. 2 ll. [Dec. 1931] [Benfolly]

Dearest Ford:

It is already late to be sending you wishes for a merry Christmas—
I have just come up for air after writing a long story ["The Captive"]
and am surprised to find that Christmas is upon us. I wonder if you
and Janice are spending it in Paris or are still at Toulon. If you are in
Paris you, being indefatigable, are probably already making plans for
half a dozen people or so. I wish we could all be together again. It
seems a long time already since the Christmas that we left Paris.

I have applied for a Guggenheim, but haven't much hopes of
getting one. They say there are ninety nine applicants this year
and Moe[1] is almost distracted. If I get one I am coming to France—
if our creditors will let us leave the country.

Perkins wrote me that they were quoting from your review of Penhally, that it was the best thing that had been said about the book yet. He wrote me some weeks ago that they had sent the review to the Bookman but that as Seward Collins came very infrequently to his office they hadn't been able to get any report on it. I suppose eventually I'll see what you have written. Why didn't you, in your well known methodical way, mail me a carbon?

I have finished a long story, which with the others I have on hand, makes enough for a book, and have proposed the volume to Perkins, who will doubtless turn it down. You would think from his letters that he didn't know where his next meal was coming from, but he is very nice to deal with. Penhally some weeks ago hadn't made back the advance so I'm not expecting anything out of it. I am trying to write some short stories, long stories, rather, and am getting a little better at it, I think, but it is very exhausting—so much harder for me than writing on a novel.

I do not see how we will ever get to New York again, for we never scrape up any money. We expect to build another cabin this spring, in the locust grove there on the way to the swimming hole. You and Janice will have to come here to see us before another year is over.

Allen and I and Andrew Lytle went to the Southern Writers' convention at the University of Virginia in October and had a grand time. It was a very funny affair, something peculiarly Southern about it from start to finish. Nothing was done, of course—it was really sort of like a gathering of second cousins who hadn't ever seen each other before but had to admit the tie of blood. Ellen Glasgow presided and set the key note for the affair. Paul Green[2] got up and said we were all going to God in a machine which incensed us agrarians, of course, but we were pretty polite about that even. We went to tea at Castle Hill—it is the first Meriwether place in this country and still so lovely. Amelie Rives[3] owns it now. She is a sort of Southern Ouida[4]—at eighty she still has the golden hair and the enormous violet eyes that set the countryside agog. She and the prince gave us the only decent liquor we had the whole time—I hope the University paid for it. They are so poor they charge fifty cents to go through the grounds. The box is wonderful, taller than trees.

I'd like to know what you think of William Faulkner's stuff. The belief seems to obtain in New York that the Southern conference was merely by way of greeting Mr. Faulkner on his way to the metropolis. Ernest Hemingway is going to be pretty sick about this boy, is already, no doubt. Faulkner was the only person at the conference who behaved like a real he-writer, reclining soddenly upon his laurels in a room at the hotel most of the time. When he did appear he was dead drunk and confined his remarks to "Yes ma'am" and "Sir?" Harrison Smith[5] attended him faithfully, ejaculating at intervals "I am here just as Bill's friend." The report is going around now that he has Bill locked up in a penthouse, Bill being unable to support his laurels in public. I am rather sorry that this young Lochinvar[6] has come out of the south and not New England. Along with his great competence he seems to have combined in him all the unadmirable qualities that New Englanders are always ascribing to the Southern mind—exactly that kind of showiness. It really all comes down to a complete lack of humility before his material. He has written a marvellous story about a negro cook who thinks her husband is going to kill her on her way home from work[7]—or it would be wonderful if he could let your flesh stop creeping long enough for you to feel the woman existing as a person.

Have you seen or heard anything of Katherine Anne Porter? She was in Germany but ought to be working her way towards Paris by this time.

I must stop and organize a little towards Christmas. The Warrens—Red has married the most horrible woman that ever I saw. It is all I can do to keep from strangling her—well, they telephoned and said they were coming for Christmas and the young man who edits The Hound and Horn and rejoices in the name of Bernard Bandler II wrote and said he was coming and one or two others. We have learned—or rather our washwoman has learned to make pretty good beer and we let the corn liquor go by and keep in that all the time, and we will have to get festive on beer or not at all.

I had a letter from Renee [Wright] not long ago and she sent Nancy a most elaborate doll trunk complete with doll, even to roller skates, for Christmas. She said that her sister, Blanche, had written to acknowledge the dedication of your other book [*When the Wicked Man*] to her but that she wasn't sure that her letter went to the right address and was fearful you might think her unappreciative. I promised to mention the matter to you when next I wrote.

Love to you both. We always miss you but more than ever at holidays. When next you come to America I wish you could arrange to settle down here for a six months or so, long enough, say, to write a book. I will type it for you. If I do get a Guggenheim we'll come to Toulon—if you all are still there, but as I say, I haven't much hope,

As ever,

C.

1. Henry Allen Moe, secretary, later president of the Guggenheim Foundation.
2. North Carolina playwright; Pulitzer Prize winner for *In Abraham's Bosom* (1927), a play about the lives of blacks.
3. Amélie Rives, Virginia-born novelist, poet, and playwright; married to the Russian Prince Troubetzkoy.
4. Marie Louise de la Ramée (1839–1908), English novelist.
5. Of Harcourt publishing house.
6. Hero of a ballad in Walter Scott's narrative poem *Marmion* (1808).
7. "That Evening Sun."

1932

CG 4. TLS. 1 l. [Early Jan. 1932] [Benfolly]

Dearest Ford:

I expected you would write something mighty good about "Penhally" but I am really a little overcome by what you did write. (I've just got the December Bookman.)[1] It is wonderful to have golden opinions from the person whose judgment you most respect—but your beautiful phrasing has worked its usual magic. What you have said will always endure in my memory. It was indeed kind of you to write the article in just the way you did. You might just have said what you thought about the book and let it go at that. I was glad that you made certain points that you did make. Particularly about certain ages of the past. They do return and loom before us and it is not always nostalgia that makes people write about them. I liked also very much what you said about the form of the novel in general. I think of it that way, too—but then my ideas about the form of the novel are derived in great part from you! You magnanimously didn't mention any of the things that are wrong with "Penhally"—but we will talk about that when we meet.

Your review, which was the first even printed word that we'd had from you in months (I haven't seen your new book)[2]—gave us a very warm feeling of your presence. All this past week when we've sat around the fire talking your name has recurred over and over again. It is strange how the absence of certain people always registers itself—you and Katherine Anne. I find that we always comment on the fact that you are not there when we have any gathering of friends.

We had a fairly quiet Christmas. The Warrens stayed with us a few days and Bernard Bandler—who with [Lincoln] Kirstein edits The Hound and Horn—came down Christmas day and stayed about a week. He is a fine fellow, quite intelligent, too—and my God, how he dotes on Henry James!

Scribner's, by the way, were enormously pleased by your review—I don't suppose it could have been more advantageously placed. Seward Collins who now refers to Allen as "Even Allen Tate" or occasionally "the more puerile Tate" so far forgot his animosity as to run two terrible pictures of me with the article.

Do write and let us have some news of you. I oughtn't to ask you to write, though. I know how correspondence weighs you down—and there is always some fool who has to be answered about something or other. You will let us know, though, if there's any chance of your coming over.

And thank you again for writing such a beautiful piece about my book,

Much love,
Caroline

By the way when Janice comes I believe we ought to be able to get her some portraits to do—by the exercise of a little discreet snobbery. We might have a little exhibit here and I'll ask a dozen people from Nashville and some from Clarksville and Hopkinsville. Those who aren't asked will be mortally offended (which will be a good thing) and those who are will feel that they have been labelled as the cognoscenti of Tennessee—that terrible woman with the black marble bathroom and all those people. If I were really sure Janice was coming I'd let myself be dragged about a little during the next few months.

1. Ford's "A Stage in American Literature" appeared in the December 1931 issue of the *Bookman*.
2. The American edition of *Return to Yesterday* was published on January 15, 1932.

CG 5. TLS. 1 l. Feb. 28 [1932] [Benfolly]

Feb. 28

Dear Ford:

Where *are* you and Janice? It is time we heard something from you—and don't tell me you're going to spend next winter in New York, for we are about to come over. I received a notification of the Guggenheim award this morning but the foundation, alas, seems to be feeling the depression and the stipend is only two thousand dollars this year. How we are going to make it I don't know but we have to accept it if only to get our debts paid here.

My fellowship doesn't go into effect until July. Our plan is to sail then and spend a few weeks in Paris and then make for some spot—cheap spot—where we can settle down and do some work. What about Toulon? Can we live there on practically nothing and just as important are you all going to be there for if you aren't there's no point in our trekking down for I can live a long time without seeing Mr. [William] Seabrook or George what's his name[1]—the one that stole Nathan's[2] countess.

We have to be somewhere where it's warm. I cannot live through another Paris winter with Allen. He had flu four times when we were there and it was terrible. We have both been ill for almost two months, incidentally, with mild cases of flu that hung on and on. I am so used to going through sieges without taking it that I was rather surprised when I came down. I am now up and walking around the yard looking at the jonquils and hyacinths in very brilliant spring sunshine and wondering if I will ever get my faculties back. Allen, too, is just about well again.

I have two novels all ready to write but God knows when I'll get a chance to write them. I got my royalty statement from "Penhally" the other day and it seems I owe them ninety six dollars on an eight hundred and fifty dollars advance. I saw that your book [*Return to Yesterday*] was a best seller on some list or other, Brentano's, I believe. I hope to God it does sell. The times seem to get worse and worse. I don't know what is going to become of us all.

I saw your poems in Poetry.[3] They are lovely. I am glad you are writing poetry again.

Do write and let us have some news of you and your plans for the fall and winter if you've got that far along. We are looking forward so to seeing you and to meeting Janice, whom I already feel that I know a little. It will be rotten luck if you are going to be on this side this winter but I have a feeling things will probably work out that way,
Much love,
Caroline

Clarksville,
Route 6

1. George Seldes; see *FMF 5*.
2. Nathan Asch; see *FMF 5*.
3. "Buckshee: Poems for 'Haitchka in France," published in the February and March 1932 issues of *Poetry*. In one of the poems, "Fleuve Profond," we learn that the name of Haïtchka is the diminutive of Schenehaia, which means "pretty creature." Saunders (2:372) adds the information that Schenehaia is Biala's Hebrew name.

FMF 6. ALS. Signed by JB. 2 ll. [Mid-Mar. 1932] Paris. Enclosed in FMF 7.

Paris Sat.
Dearest Caroline:
    What glorious news![1]

I was just stepping out of the house intending to come here (the Select) & write this to you while Janice was taking a bath—our geyser having struck!—at the Bains de l'Observatoire when your letter was handed to me by the concierge. (We have a new concierge, Mme Jeanne having become lady's maid to Barbara Harrison!)[2]

I don't really know where to begin, there being such a complication of news. Firstly, then, I was determined not to write to you till we had better news . . . from wh. you may deduce that we do have better news & also that we have been having a pretty bad time for long enough. To begin with Smith turned out a complete crook (T.R.S. of Liveright)[3] and although my books have been bestsellers has paid me practically nothing so that we have actually been short of food, sometimes for longish periods. We cd have stood it at Toulon but, with the collapse of the £ Stella became practically penniless so we had to lend her & Julie the Toulon place where she has lived on what she got by renting her studio. So we had to come up to 32 [rue de Vaugirard] & stick things out as well as we could. Now, suddenly, Stella has got four portraits to paint in N.Y. & is leaving for that city on the 18th. So we have to go down to Toulon to look after Julie who is going to school there. *But* on Monday last Ray Long[4] turned up & signed a contract to take all my work for three years with monthly payments that will make us quite comfortable. Have you got all that.

Well then: we are now waiting for his first payment, next week, before going down to T[oulon]. In the meantime we are kept quite busy negotiating with Katherine Anne & Ellen Crow[5] to lend them 32. Katherine Anne is in the hotel next door which is expensive & where she never sees the sun, whereas we have sunlight all day long. (We are in the apt. that Stella used to have, not your old one.) Ellen Crow has been unable to pay any rent for six months & is penniless. Yet it is more difficult to lend them that apartment than it wd. be if we wanted $500 a month for it.

What a pity you are not coming sooner, because we *think* of giving up the apt. in July. But wait. I can be more definite when 'Aitchka comes in, clean. We *plan* to stay in Toulon till October–Nov. & then go to N.Y. for the winter. That might fit in with yr plans all right. For if you came there about July by October you might have had enough of us & be prepared—à la Willie Seabrook!—to throw us out & occupy our nest yourselves.

Janice is now here & shall continue
Dear Caroline
I am a dour & sour Russian pessimist so have no words with which to tell you how glad I am you've got the scholarship & are

coming over. But we are so hungry for friends (not intimate acquaintances) that I wish you would come sooner, if only for Ford's sake. But he says that if I suggested that you come right away & live in our apartment that you would spend all your money & have none with which to come down to Toulon. Is that true? But if it is impossible we will find you a house in Toulon & Ford says that we will see to it that you live within your means. He's awfully good that way about other people's incomes.

He really has been trying to write you for a long time, but there was nothing but bad news to tell, tho we were awfully touched at your offering to get me a show in Tennessee & bring yourself out to pay visits with that end in view. But we also found the idea hilariously funny, as I never paint any portraits any more because of the trouble I get into with indignant relatives. I painted the little sketch of Julie in an off moment, and if you look closely you will see that even that hasn't the slightest resemblance to her. But the fact is that no Southern gentleman would tolerate any portrait I painted of any of his relations. We'd all be ridden out of town on a rail.

I've got myself rather sidetracked with the above sentiments & can't think what I wanted to say. Anyway Katherine Anne came to Paris about a month ago for a few days, went to Spain for forever & turned up again 2 days later minus a lot of money & sleep. She's as mad as a hatter & Ford is in a perfect fever of maternal anxiety about her, & even I've been stung a little by the same insect. I've been trying to make her come down to Toulon, & tho each time I spoke of it she rushed off to pack, she finally only moved next door to us. She is a dear.

What I always meant to say if I ever wrote you was: *why* did you wish the Trasks on Ford? I knew Willard myself for about 5 years & it was too much finding him on the scene again but he, delighted, with the double claim he now has on us, (& Mary, for deah Willahd's sake I suppose, loves us too,) is making our lives miserable. It's only advice he wants, but I never knew *anybody* who needed as much advice as that. From diapers to Donne. What does he do with it all?

(I forgot to say that Ford thinks you ought to take a boat from New Orleans to Marseilles straight & not stop anywhere where you can spend your money. He also disapproves of all I'm saying so I'm quitting. I'm glad you think you know me a little. I feel the same.) Janice

1. About Gordon's Guggenheim Fellowship.
2. A wealthy American who ran a small publishing firm in Paris together with Monroe Wheeler.

3. T. R. Smith of the publishing firm Liveright.
4. Of Long and Smith, the American publisher of *The Rash Act*.
5. Presumably Helen Crowe; cf. *FMF 4*.

FMF 7. TLS. 2 ll. [Apr. 23, 1932] Toulon.

St George's Day alias Shakespeare's Birthday
Dearest Caroline,

I am not such a criminal as I may seem for not having ere this despatched the enclosed [*FMF 6*] which must have been written six weeks ago. I was determined not to write till I could be calm or at least cheerful and the same evening as that on which Janice and I concocted the enclosed a series of alarums and excursions[1] began and have practically not yet ended. I suppose they never do. It seemed to culminate whilst we were trying to have a day or two's holiday in Tarascon by our having all our available money blown into the Rhone. This sounds improbable but if you knew what the wind called the mistral is like by the corner of the castle of the good king René you would understand. At any rate the bewilderment and incredulity with which one saw Janice's bag flying out of her hands and opening in mid-air with all our notes of all sorts of dimensions up to frs 500 buzzing out on the air like a swarm of bees—that amazement and incredulity were something in which you could hardly be expected to believe. So we had to give up our holiday—which we terribly needed because we were both worn out and come straight on here with as it were our tails between our legs.

Then of course began a sort of martyrdom with the house overfull with Julie and a secretary and ourselves and only room for two really and the femme de ménage going into hospital for appendicitis and Julie having to be got off to school at seven and so on and so on and the mistral blowing all day for a month like liquid ice and I having to get a piece of work finished in a desperate hurry and the secretary—who is a little atom, male, about four foot two—in hysterics all the time. However, after a hell of a month, we have now got a femme de ménage who is really a miracle—an immense, blonde Italian—and we have had two days of real Mediterranean spring weather (though this morning it is actually raining, a thing it has never been known to do in mid-April. But that may help the garden and prevent drought in June) and I am getting to the end of my novel [*The Rash Act*] and Janice has managed to do some work and Mr [Richard] Murphy has had no hysterics for quite two days and the cat (Siamese called Sirocco) has not miauled for over half an hour and getting Julie off to school has become almost a mechanical operation and Ray Long pay up regularly. So, for the moment, that is almost what could be called human felicity. Of course I have contracted—what I never had before—an almost complete insomnia, but I combat it with drugs and carry on.

Katherine Anne finally decided to instal herself at 32 having spent all her money and the first fire she had lit tons of bricks came falling down the chimney and police and firemen and the sanitary squad rushed in, so we are faced with all sorts of fines and amorcements and prosecutions,[2] and the bath geyser went wrong and the femme de ménage whom we considered an angel did not suit her. But things I suppose must be. . . . And now she or someone connected with her has come into some money and I got her a little job which as far as I know she is doing.[3] So I have hopes that that part of the hide may be lying down.

Anyhow that is the way the world goes here—and I suppose that in the solid South they do not go very differently.

We reiterate all the urgings to come here that are contained in the previous message. After the 14th July when Julie goes off on her holidays we might even be able to offer you hospitality if not of bed then at least of board. But if you contemplate coming here let us know soon because by July every room in every farm-house for miles around is occupied by summer boarders. Pray do come.

For myself I am finishing a novel that I think this time really does [Henry] James's trick of "uniting to considerable skill enviable possibilities of popularity." In revenge I am convinced—as I always am—that I shall drop dead before it is finished so that it will have no value. But the same emotions overcome me every time I am near finishing a book so I suppose they have no particular significance.

And you? I wish I could keep more in contact with your work. The sales of PENHALLY do not seem to have been very satisfactory. I suppose that has, like everything else, to be put down to the Crisis but it is none the less disappointing.

Janice and Julie send their loves to you and Nancy who, I suppose, has by now quite forgotten all her French and my respects go to Allen some of whose enviable activities reach me by way of POETRY and other organs.

And so: God guard you; God guide you; God watch over you at your goings out and your comings in from the same!

Yours always
FMF

1. Calls to arms and raids.
2. Investigations (?) and prosecutions. Apparently Ford slipped up on his French in the invention of the word "amorcements."

3. Translating a selection of French songs for the firm Harrison of Paris; a
limited edition titled *Katherine Anne Porter's French Song Book* (1933) was
released.

CG 6. TLS. 1 l. [May 13, 1932] [Merry Mont]

Dear Ford and Janice:

We have just got a cable from John Ransom. The Carnegie Foundation is sending a professor over so Allen won't get the teaching
job after all. This means we'll spend the winter in France, and no
doubt Toulon.

Chink and Lyle Lanier[1] are coming down with us, so if you come
across any available lodgings engage some for them too. They won't
be there very long, however, as they have to come back in September to Vanderbilt. And as I said before please don't take two steps
out of your way for any of us as we can surely find some place to
live after we get there. If you all do go to New York in the fall you
might like to rent your place to us—but I hope you won't go and
shall try to prevail on you not to.

I have been re-reading your letter, the hand written part. You
say "we think of giving up the apartment in July" but that means of
course the Paris apartment, and obviously it is given up—we don't
want to rush down to Toulon especially to see you all and find you
on the point of rushing somewhere else.

This, I believe, is all the news from us and again doesn't require
any acknowledgement. We just wanted to let you know we were
coming four and a half strong, counting Nancy.

love,
C.

The Lindbergh baby was found dead on the estate yesterday,
buried under some leaves.[2] It is so pitiful.

1. Friends from Nashville; Chink Lanier was Andrew Lytle's cousin.
2. The baby was found on May 12, 1932. In 1934 Bruno Hauptmann was arrested
   for the murder of Charles A. Lindbergh's son and executed in 1936.

CG 7. TLS. 2 ll. June 18 [1932] Merry Mont.

Merry Mont
June 18

Dearest Ford:

Your letter[1] came some days ago. I have been waiting to answer it
till I knew something more definite about our plans but I don't know
any more now than I did when the letter came. You and Janice are too
hospitable. We could not think of crowding in on you. But we hope to

get lodgings somewhere near you. The villa in the bottom of your garden is the most attractive prospect of course, but the price seems a bit steep. I fear prices haven't fallen there as much as they have in this country. We rented our house furnished complete down to electric refrigerator and apparatus for making beer, as well as labor to produce a garden for thirty five dollars a month and thought we were lucky. Things seem to get worse and worse here. It is really alarming. I am glad to get out of the country for a while for even if the French are suffering I don't understand the language very well and can't suffer much with them. And to think that there is nobody in Toulon as far as I know that is kin to us! That is something to look forward to. I have been having the most frightful time with Dad who has just come up from Florida, trying to make him preserve a semblance of decency towards the kin. Of course Aunt Molly Ferguson's funeral has to come off while he's here, and he won't go to it. Says he "Cousin Molly Ferguson is no more kin to me than a catfish and I am not going to her funeral." I had just got Allen to the point where he was fairly decent to them but Dad's example incited him to rebellion and he too goes around proclaiming that he is not kin to any of them. It's really been hectic here, what with meeting trains and hauling ice and sheep and niggers from one place to the other. But I haven't felt well enough to work much anyhow, so it hasn't made much difference.

To return to our plans. We are in a stew now trying to decide whether or not to leave Nancy. Her fond great aunt [Margaret Meriwether Campbell] in Chattanooga is very anxious to have her stay and of course it would [make] everything much simpler for us. I can't bear the idea of forcing her to stay if she doesn't want to, though it would probably be much better for her. If she isn't with us Allen and I will just take a cheap room somewhere. I would love to get out of the cares of a menage for a year. I am so tired of planning meals and so on. I know I could get a lot more work done.

Well, we are coming anyhow, with or without Nancy, in or out of our right minds. If Nancy comes we'll have to take a villa, but I'm afraid to make any decision on it now which is why we haven't cabled as you suggested.

Many thanks to both of you for troubling yourselves about our affairs. We will not require as much advice as Willard [Trask] when we finally get there! And we are looking forward so to seeing you. And I am dying to read your novel [*The Rash Act*]. It ought to be nearly finished by now. I am sorry about the insomnia. I hope it is better now. It's writing a book makes you have it.

I have just realized that we are leaving here very soon, around July 1. But we are stopping along the way to visit and as Louis

Untermeyer[2] is always saying to sing for our supper. *I* am going to lecture at Monteagle on Southern novelists! I am scared to death but they say the audience is always old ladies with palm leaf fans who never change their expression no matter what you say.

If you should write again soon address us in care of the Guggenheim Foundation, 551 Fifth Ave. Will be in New York from the eighteenth to the twenty first—I'm going to try to see Stella. After July 21 address us Guaranty Trust in Paris,

Love,

Caroline

Allen has written (by request!) a poem for the Confederate veterans' reunion in Richmond![3] I don't imagine the veterans will like it much, though, as he asserts that "all men now are Yankees in the country of the damned."

1. This letter is missing.
2. Versatile writer, well-known for his anthologies, e.g., *Modern American Poetry* (1919; often revised).
3. "The Secret of the Captain (The Night before the Reunion)," revised as "To the Lacedemonians."

CG 8. TLS. 1 l. [Early Aug.? 1932] Paris.

Dearest Ford:

We have just got in—it is so much easier to drive into Paris than it is to drive into New York. We stopped at Lavignes's and had dinner and then came to 32. I was nerving myself to converse with a strange concierge when out pops Mme Jeanne and her aunt and much going on and interchange of va biens and all of us very glad to see each other. And how nice it is to be here and you all were darlings to think of it and leave the letter for us. Oh, I am so glad to be here!

Mme Jeanne confides that Katherine Anne is not a good house-keeper and indeed she isn't—except by fits and starts. She wrote me from Switzerland that she was coming over to meet us but no signs of her here—or at least no letter!—and at the Savoy they say she is parti many months.

We have had our dinner and a drink or two at the Brasserie de l'Odeon and Allen and Sally Wood have gone off to buy the ticket for the Clarksville jeune fille[1] whom we intend to ship to Switzerland tomorrow and high time for she fell in love with a young German "creator of machinery" on the boat and says bitterly every now and then that she has no interest in France. We are not quite sure when we will get to Toulon so don't have us on your mind and go ahead and finish up the vacation—I hope it punctuates a book.

We left Nancy in Chattanooga—did I tell you. Every time I step out on the street I am afraid I will meet Mme Gau who will not approve, I am sure. We are missing her horribly but I don't know what we'd have done with her along. We had two or maybe it was three hectic days in New York. I remember being whirled round and round the Empire State building which certainly is something to look at and then rushing to Bernard Bandler's apartment getting there just in time to tune in on Allen reading his poems on the radio. It was very funny. We all sat on the floor in front of so to speak Allen and as the guests came in and heard Allen booming forth they all sort of collapsed in corners. Bernard kept asking us who we wanted to see but everybody was out of town so he thought the guests up himself—a strange assortment, including Coby Gilman[2] and Muriel Draper.[3] I don't mean they came together, but why he should have thought we wanted to see either of them. Muriel Draper took a look at Malcolm Cowley and said "Why, there's Pierre Loving"[4] which ought to hold Malcolm for a while. I seem to have heard bits of news in New York but I can't remember any of it. We have been on the road so long.

I keep striking the wrong keys but I am writing by one dim light. Being so dumb about things I can't figure how to plug in your table lamp and Allen is still off buying that ticket. This is just to let you know that we are here and how much we want to see you both.

Much love, c.

In the morning: I've finally got a chance to exchange a few words with Allen. He comes forth with the news that he is already overdue with two articles for the New Republic. He says he will have to sit down and write them immediately. So I think we'll let the Laniers take our car and go on south and wait here till their return two or three weeks from now. That would put us in Toulon around the first of September—but you must not have us on your minds or change your plans in any way for us.

1. Dorothy Ann Ross, a distant cousin of Gordon.
2. Coburn (Coby) Gilman, an American writer associated with *Travel* magazine.
3. A poet, who with her husband, the singer Paul Draper, was known for holding a literary salon in New York.
4. American author and editor of plays, among them *The Stick-Up: A Rough-Neck Fantasy* (1922).

CG 9. **CG to JB. TLS. 1 l. [Sept.? 1932] Toulon.**

For God's sake read this one first.

Dear Janice:

Your letter[1] just came. I hope you have solved the studio problem by this time—it must be a frightful ordeal. But no doubt you are off to Germany—or Rome—by this time.

We go tomorrow to Les Hortensias. I hate to leave and have just been wandering around the garden for a farewell look. It has been so lovely here—and we have got more work done in this week than in the last six. I like—or rather I dislike doing the house work here less than any place I've ever lived. It sort of does itself—of course I don't cook the enormous dinners that Ford does. I haven't had Charlotte—I really haven't needed her, though.

The chickens are all well and are enjoying their turn in the garden just now. The hens are very nice and lay an egg for our breakfast almost every morning. We had a grand rain last night that soaked the garden. For once in my life I've had all the eggplant I want. There is an enormous melon ripe now, which you, alas, will never see, and two or three others coming on and a few minutes ago I found a yellow orange. That big cucumber vine has had a renaissance and suddenly produced a lot of cucumbers which I eat up as fast as they come.

Shalammis scared me to death by disappearing two days—down at the Pats,[2] of course. I do not think he really has a nice nature. He catches field mice and tortures them under the bed where I am trying to take a nap, then comes out looking exceptionally beautiful and wants to take a nap with me.

There is absolutely no news from us—except that we have finally had news from Bernard [Bandler] and Nancy, both of whom we were worried about. Nancy seems to have been spending her time in the Country Club pool and Bernard has been in Switzerland. His address is the National City Bank unless he's gone back. I still hope you all will get in touch with him—he'd be so pleased to see you. *We* have seen nobody but M. Dupont who is very attentive—I foresee that I will never shatter the bond forged between us this week.

Tell Ford not to worry about his precious chickens. I will take as good care of them as I can. I'll come down in the afternoon early enough for them to get a run in the garden and perhaps I can get the Pats to shut them up at night. I wish we could stay here till you all get back but Mme Lamure[3] seems anxious to get us in and Sally and Allen say they want to get settled. Allen is still in the throes of his short story[4] and I have outlined every chapter of my novel [*The Garden of Adonis*] so that it should click into place like something by Mr. Faulkner. It is exactly a year ago today that I wrote the first two paragraphs of that novel and have never been able to add another paragraph to them.

Goodbye. Have a grand time. Love to you both,

c.

1. This letter is missing.
2. M. le Vicomte and Mme la Vicomtesse de la Pastellière, Ford's neighbors in Toulon.
3. Gisette Lamure, owner of Villa les Hortensias.
4. "The Immortal Woman," later included in the novel *The Fathers* (1938).

CG 10. CG to JB. TLS. 1 l. [Sept.? 1932] Toulon.

My dear Janice:

The enclosed letter was written before the happenings of the last two days! I shall now recount *them* in order. On the day that we were moving to Les Hortensias the bell rang and a girl named Ruth Harris[1] appeared. She had just come from the [William and Katie] Seabrooks and had been wandering around the Chemin du Fort trying to find the Villa Paul. I asked her to sit down and have some figs, then I asked her to stay to lunch, then when I found out she was spending the night at the Hotel du Port I asked her to spend the night at the Villa Paul instead. She accepted these various invitations, then having installed herself for the night said she believed she'd stay a few days and go over a manuscript or something and did I think it would be all right with you all. I told her I was sure it would and was pleased to have somebody on the place.

Well . . . yesterday afternoon we all went down to that picnic place and swam, then Miss Harris and I went back to the Villa Paul and watered the garden and fed the chickens. The chickens were taking their turn in the garden and averse to going home but we shooed them all in around six o'clock and went on up to Les Hortensias where we had dinner. At ten o'clock we escorted Miss Harris back to the Villa Paul, lit some candles and gave her a flash light and left her to spend the night alone. (I wouldn't have done it for anything in the world but I've been reading horror stories.) This morning very early came a wild tingling on the bell and in burst Miss Harris. When we asked what in the name of God had happened she said hysterically that she didn't know but that something had happened to the chickens. She said she had heard squawkings in the night but had been too scared to investigate. She and I then went down to the villa and found every single chicken dead. They simply lay there in the coops dead, as if their necks were broken—all except the sitting hen who has escaped somewhere. There was not a drop of blood to be seen anywhere, the bodies of the chickens all intact except that the mammy cat had eaten a very little of one chicken. The strange thing, too, is that the door of the coop which

I had shut most carefully was opened, I swear as if by a hand! The pin, for instance, which fastens the hens' coop seemed to have been *taken* out. I remarked on this, Watson, but thought no more of it at the time. I then thought of M. Durant's dog. We descended to that villa and interviewed M. Durant who said his dog had been at home all night—I wanted him to know about it, anyway, though we made no accusation, of course.

Mme Pat was wild over the news, of course, and made one suggestion that sounds weird though I find myself returning to it. She thinks it was Charlotte—"la vengeance" etc. and the Italians will do anything. It sounds fantastic but the conditions of the coops was indeed strange. A weasel doesn't eat the chicken but simply sucks the blood from the throat. A fox eats part of the body, but these chickens simply lay there without a drop of blood visible anywhere. Also a beast would never open the doors. The door of the little chickens' coop was pushed open—the door of the hens' coop shut but with the pin that fastens it slipped out.

I suppose it will always remain a mystery but my God it is a cruel thing to happen. My sympathies are divided equally with Ford and the chickens.

Miss Harris is pretty hysterical. She is going to sleep here tonight and will work and eat at the villa. I suppose it is a good thing to have somebody there during the day even if we can't persuade her to stay at night. I trust it is all right turning the place over to somebody else? I thought innocently that it would be fine to have somebody there to look after things—but of course she was too frightened in the night to go down to see what was happening. Mme Pat says they heard the squawkings too, but I suppose they thought we were still there—they were away when we left.

We carried the canary to Mme Pat this morning—I don't want his poor little blood on my hands.

I can't tell you how sorry I am and I know this news is going to depress you. I would save it—about the chickens—but if Mme Pat is right and it is somebody I thought you ought to know in case anything was stolen from the house. Miss Harris has asked a friend to come and stay a week—I trust that too is all right?—and if there are the two of them they will sleep at the villa which will be better, I think.

It is now nearly noon and we have just completed the circle, M. Durant, Mme Pat and so on and much voluble advice, of course, from Mme Lamure. Also a very handsome young workman left his work on the adjacent villa to examine and inter the chickens for us. Quite a morning, all in all and I come home and open my American mail and my aunt starts off by recounting the death of our little puppy and then goes on to tell how the police dog has bitten a motor cop—of all people—and will have to be retired to the country.

Shalammis and the canary seem to be in excellent health but God knows what the morrow will bring.

I am sorry to be the bearer of such bad news—I suppose I really ought to have kept it from you but the responsibility is too much for me.

Love and please give Ford my deepest sympathy about the chickens. Miss Harris—and we too, of course—want to replace them but what we are pondering now is whether Ford can get attached to the new chickens. "He loved them like his children" said Mme Pat—find out whether he would prefer to find chickens in the coop or pick them out himself, please.

Yours most dejectedly,
caroline

Allen says we ought to have taken finger prints. We are all still puzzling over the mystery!

1. Poet-friend of Stella Bowen.

CG 11. TLS. 1 l. [Nov. 1932] Paris.

Dearest Janice and Ford:

We're settled after the usual alarums at 37 rue Denfert-Rochereau,[1] paying of course more than we expected to, but it's a very pleasant place. This finding a place with the petite cuisine attached is a desperate business. This place is on the ground floor of a back court, no running water, heat it with a stove and so on, but it's really very pleasant. It is a studio with a little kitchen and the usual dark balcony bedroom, but the studio itself is very pleasant. Five hundred francs. The rue Daguerre places were all taken and the Servandoni people wanted five hundred francs for two closets up six flights of stairs—But I will spare you the details of our sufferings.

Driving around in our search we suddenly found ourselves on an impasse which turned out to be rue Boissonade. We dashed in a moment and found Stella and Julie at home. Julie, sitting up in bed, reading and looking it seemed to me exactly like Ford if he were thirteen years old and more feminine in appearance. I had not seen her since her hair was cut—it makes the likeness more apparent.

The weather is very mild now but we haven't seen the sun since we left Valence. The trip as far as there was perfectly marvellous, the country is incredibly beautiful now. We were cursing all the way because you didn't come. If I had only made a quart or so of hot coffee and poured it down your throats you would have leaped out of that bed and come along, I know. We stopped at Arles and saw the Roman arena. The tomb of the consuls strikes me even more. Those poplar trees and rows of gray tombs and the ground covered with yellow leaves. It's so beautiful at this time of year. There was a large man sitting with his back to us talking to a small lady and we said "My God, they've come after all" and went rushing down to confront two French people, of course! The light was going when we got to Tarascon and there was a mist all around the castle but we picked out exactly the spot from which you painted the castle. We spent the night at Avignon—at the Hotel Louvre, rue Sainte Agricole, which is the best small hotel I ever struck, twenty francs for a good room. We saw the Palace of the Popes in the morning. An incredibly bright, golden day—the country is so lovely from those ramparts—I could hardly bear to leave it. That was the last sight we've had of the sun. It got darker and darker from Avignon on. We drove half a day, crawling through a fog at about ten miles an hour. And of course there is the usual November weather here.

We've spent one evening at the Closerie des Lilas and we're dining tonight with the [John Peale] Bishops but aside from these occasions we haven't been anywhere or seen anybody. Helen Crowe says she saw in the paper where Gene's boss had been transferred to Paris which means I suppose that Katherine Anne is here now or will be here soon. K.A. would never desert Mr. Micawber—if he was on his way to Paris!

We spent two days cleaning this place. It was filthy. And now we have our typewriters set up and it really looks as if we might get to work. I feel rather silly having all this painting light going to waste and you worrying along with the sun streaming on you. If we could just change for a few hours a day!

Not having seen anybody and God willing not going to see anybody I have no news to report. We'll keep on the lookout, of course, for studios. The landlord says there may be a vacancy here by the first of next month. It is a very nice location. The front house has been improved and is of course expensive but the studios on the back court are much cheaper.

Must stop and dress. Love and many thanks for your noble

efforts in getting us [a place]. Be sure and come up as soon as you can. It doesn't seem right here without you,

as ever,

C.

1. This letter ends with a penciled map of the location of the studio.

CG 12. CG to JB. TL. 1 l. [Late Dec. 1932] Paris.

Dear Janice:

I write hurriedly of business matters. We are giving up this studio today or tomorrow—we have found a pension where we can live, the two of us, for sixty dollars a month. It will be as cheap if not cheaper than this place and it will mean a lot to me to be relieved of any housework. I have not had a femme de menage to do even the cleaning here.

It is almost impossible to pick out living quarters for anybody else but I feel I ought to tell you about this place if you are really coming up in January. We have walked miles, looked at every furnished studio we came across and this one is by far the best we've seen. Walter Lowenfels,[1] who fancies himself now as a real estate agent wants to take it over when we leave. He says he could get six hundred for it. We complained that it was expensive to heat—it is—and they have reduced the rent to four hundred and fifty a month. I have looked at a good many little studios for three fifty and they are dingy holes compared to this. I will describe it to you and you can think it over/

The studio is good sized, larger than Cecil's[2] barn-studio, with a petite cuisine and a balcony bedroom. The petite cuisine is on the order of the one you have at Villa Paul, the balcony bedroom is dark but you can keep clothes there and it is a splendid place to take baths, hot air rising the way it does! There is no running water—you get it in the court—and you heat the place with a little stove. We have been very warm here, as warm as I care to be. The studio itself is pleasant— it was furnished by a painter who got broke and had to leave, so it doesn't have any of the ordinary furnished room aspect. There are plenty of comfortable chairs, screens, tables and so on, hangings which though worn are yet passable. The large mural is trying but we mostly turn our backs on it. There is plenty of light. And the place is on the ground floor of a back court—nice little garden. The house in front is quite swank, iron grills and marble stairs etc. but these studios in the back, not having confort moderne are cheap. I mean by this that it is a good address and the studio itself is a place where you could ask people to see your pictures. There is no extra room for Ford to work in but the studio itself is so large that he, the smallest guinea pig might well retire behind a screen and nobody would even know he was there if he wouldn't cheer.

I am setting all these details down so conscientiously because I really feel that you can hardly do better at the price. Two years ago this place rented for seven hundred and fifty francs a month. As I say we have looked at places and places and found nothing that even compared with this.

We are giving up the place in the next day or two anyhow. I am right in the midst of another short story ["Old Red"] and must get settled and back to work. (I sold Tom Rivers to the Yale Review.)[3] I wish you all were coming up sooner. If you are interested in this place telegraph us at the Guaranty Trust Co. If you want to hold the place we will come over and pay a deposit on it—Lowenfels insists that it will go quickly, but of course you never know about that. Anyhow I wanted youall to have the benefits—if any—of our researches.

We are moving mostly because we are as usual running short of money and getting into a pension now we won't have to pay till our next Guggenheim installment is due. Also the pension is a little cheaper.

Allen wrote the Guggenheims about you in the strongest terms he could—haven't heard anything from Moe yet.

Must give this to Allen to mail.

Love and belated birthday wishes to Ford.[4] We all remembered his birthday but it found us all broke as usual. We hardly managed to drink his health. We ate dinner with K. A. and Gene at their pension—since we could charge the dinner—then having some ten francs between us we went to the Capoulade and drank the ten francs up except for seventy five cen'mes or so. Not having enough to buy a package of cigarettes we went down to that place on the Odeon where there are gambling machines, shot our centimes and won enough to buy a package of cigarettes which we divided between the four of us. You can see what a gay life we're leading!

1. American poet, newspaperman, editor, and critic.
2. Cecil Wright, English painter; was a friend of Sally Wood; he did a portrait of Gordon in November 1932.
3. The story "Tom Rivers" appeared in the October 1933 issue of the *Yale Review*.
4. Ford's birthday was December 17.

1933

Monday

Dear Janice:

I was just getting ready to write you about the things you'd need for the studio. We went by Christmas Eve and paid them a hundred francs to hold it. I had told them vehemently that my friends would not take it unless everything was made propre and they swore they'd brush carpets and so on. It was dark when we got there and I couldn't get the right light to work but it looked as though they had spent some time on it. The place needed cleaning terribly. As for what you need there is one pair of sheets and pillow cases there, enough blankets for one bed but not quite enough for two. There are a good many plates, a sizable tea pot, plenty of glasses of a sort, two cups and a few vegetable dishes. I have bought a few things which you can have—a little oven, two earthenware baking dishes and I can let you have knives and forks too. But be sure and bring sheets and towels and some cups unless you want to buy them. Stella had lent us a fine collection of useful objects, slop jars, ewers, sauce pans etc. We returned them but I will get them back as soon as she returns from England. With what there is between us you could get by for a few months without buying anything I should say. Oh, I bought a broom. We'll make those hell hounds return it if they've taken it. We left enough coal there for a week, but they've probably taken it as I gave no orders for its disposition. Anyway we'll have some there for you.

While I think about it no, we haven't drawn on that twenty we paid you back. And no, don't send us a cheque for the deposit. We had plenty. I'm glad to get a little more paid on our debt to you.

I seem to remember sending you all a drunken post card from the Cochon de Lait where we had dinner with K. A. Gene and as Allen says Hellion Crowe Christmas Eve. We went on from there to help dress the Lowenfels child's tree and didn't get to midnight mass because the Lowenfels were so slow and I remember onion soup somewhere after that but Christmas this year has been rather vague for me, not because I've drunk much. Rather I've gone it through like the dormouse, waking only at intervals. Each place I went I picked out a soft spot and went to sleep and Allen would haul me up and set me on my feet when the time came to move. Finally I broke down and treated myself to a whole day in bed. Since when I have a little more idea of what's going on.

Little John Untermeyer[1] is recovered, though the doctors have never been able to diagnose his mysterious ailment. Nancy has flu or had when my aunt wrote but very mildly and her fever had already gone to normal the last bulletin that came. Julie lost seven kilos during her attack of flu, Stella says, but she is beginning to pick up and was quite animated when I saw her last, Friday evening, just before they left. I cannot think of any more news. We are so glad you all are coming. If you have time drop us a card naming the time of day of your arrival. If it's cold we'd like to have a fire going before you come.

Gertrude Stein and Miss Toklas[2] are reading Faulkner. Miss Toklas says she is just too excited over the story of Sanctuary which she hears is very interesting. Gertrude told Allen she was sorry he had given up writing poetry as he seemed to know something about it.

Katherine Anne was feeling swell when she arrived but is already cracking a little under the strain of a Paris winter. But she still looks a thousand times better than she did when I saw her last.

I do hope you won't find the studio too inconvenient. I think you can keep warm there and have a decent light for painting, and there is room for one's friends to turn about when they come to see you. More I cannot say for it.

Allen sends his love. We will be looking for you Monday,

Love, c.

There is a tea-kettle and coffee pot at the studio but no frying pan. The cooking utensils consist of two sauce pan and a shallow pan suitable for poaching eggs & for nothing else in God's world. But Stella had several sauce pans to lend.

Bring: sheets

          pillow cases

          towels

          (extra blanket if you want two beds. One

          three quarter bed in studio, one single bed on

          balcony)

pitcher
spoons, perhaps knives & forks. I have
only a few.

1. Son of Louis Untermeyer.
2. At Gertrude Stein's literary salon in Paris, it was her companion Alice
   B. Toklas's job to entertain the lady visitors, while the hostess devoted
   herself to the men.

CG *14*. ALS. 1 l. [Feb. 21, 1933] Hampton Roads, Va.

Tuesday

Dearest Janice and Ford:

This is to apprise you that we have lived through the voyage,
rather to my surprise. It hasn't been any worse than usual, I suppose. We're in Hampden Roads now—the sky line of Norfolk is
very different from that of New York. Allen was up early to see
Cape Henry and the other Cape whatever it is, trying to imagine
how it all looked to Captain John Smith[1]—pretty swell, I think.

We're going to stop in Maryland with Phelps Putnam for a week:
"Mirival," Sandy Spring, Maryland the address is—then on to
Merry Mont.

When we got to Le Havre the first person we saw was Virginia
Moore,[2] bag and baggage! I never thought she'd make it—but on
the other hand of course she would!

We thought of youall cooking all day that next Sunday—that
chicken will always dwell in my memory but it was fortunate that we
left when we did. We were driving till two o'clock in the morning,
mostly around Rouen. We met dozens of cheerful, intoxicated people
who carefully directed us off the national route, running beside the car
for some distance sometimes to set us on the wrong road.

Virginia says tell youall she was so sorry not to see you again.
John [Untermeyer] is blowing his horn so loudly in my ear I can't
write. And there's no news from us. Do write and let us know how
everything goes,

Love,
C.

Route One
Trenton, Kentucky

1. As one of a group of colonists, Capt. John Smith (1580–1631) disem-
   barked at Jamestown in May 1607.
2. Louis Untermeyer's wife.

CG 15. TLS. 1 l. Feb. 27, 1933. [Sandy Spring, MD?]

27.2.33
Ford Madox Ford Esq
37 rue Denfert Rochereau
Paris V.
France.

Dear Ford,

As we are leaving for Kentucky tomorrow will you please act for me about the English rights of PENHALLY?

I am sure you can get as good terms as anyone else could from Cape or from any one else if he does not want the book and, as we are going to be so far away it would take an immense time for me to negotiate directly with any English publisher.

Perhaps you would also negotiate if possible some sort of terms for my next book [*The Garden of Adonis*] which I have been writing here.

You know all about it. I expect to have it finished by mid-Fall if we find things all right at home.

Thanks
Caroline Gordon Tate

CG 16. CG to JB. TLS. 1 l. Mar. 11 [1933] Merry Mont.

March 11

Dearest Janice:

I was awfully glad to get your letter.[1] I found a letter here from Perkins saying that the Atlantic Monthly wanted Ford's article.[2] We have telegraphed Ellery Sidgwick[3] Ford's address just to be on the safe side though I imagine they are already in communication. I am glad to hear he's made a connection with Lippincott. I hope business worries are off your mind as a result.

You said in your letter that you enclosed a telegram but there was no telegram in the letter. What was it?

I almost fainted when I heard that Moe was sending another $ 250. I suppose he'll send it by cheque. I know that if you all need money you need it—or have needed it—this last week. I could lend you some if I could get my hands on some that's coming in. But we landed here with not one cent left after we'd paid those damn taxes. Allen had told me he sent the cheque before we left but he hadn't. However he was able to come back with "How would we have got home?" when I re-proached him with the deceit.

We had a fairly good trip—only one day of rough weather—

spent four days in Maryland with Phelps Putnam, then on to Chattanooga where we spent two days with Nancy and the rest of the family. Nancy has grown a lot and has grown touchingly polite. She sits up and reads like a grown person. We decided to leave her there to finish the school year.

We arrived at Merry Mont three days ago. I've been trying ever since to sit down to a typewriter but haven't got settled yet. Life here is very distracting. I think we will stay here for the next six months. My grandmother is very anxious for us to and our house is rented till October anyway.

Allen is going to town and wants to mail all the letters. Will write later/

Love for both of you, c.

I've just figured out what the "other telegram" you mentioned must be. From Perkins again. *Please,* if any mail comes there for us forward it to us at

"Merry Mont"
Trenton, Kentucky

1. This letter is missing.
2. "Contrasts: Memories of John Galsworthy and George Moore" appeared in the May 1933 issue of *Atlantic Monthly*.
3. Ellery Sedgwick, editor of the *Atlantic Monthly*.

CG 17. CG to JB. TLS. 2 ll. Mar. 15 [1933] Merry Mont.

March 15
Merry Mont
Trenton, Ky.

Dearest Janice:

Your second letter has just come.[1] The N[ew] R[epublic] cable was not important—I should never have forgiven you if you'd wasted a cable on it in these parlous times. I left those few francs not for a cable but thinking they *might* come in handy if there was an hiatus between payments. I am wondering how in the devil you all are making out. I certainly hope you've located somebody who can lend you some cash. We're dead broke as usual and are sitting here hoping that Moe's cheque will come sooner or later. I don't like to write him about it as I'm not supposed to be in this country yet.

I suppose we're really better off than any of us right now. The moratorium has been a great convenience to us except for not having cash for small expenses. The bank had to admit sadly that they couldn't hound us about our note for awhile yet and one or two other little things were staved off. In the meantime we can live indefinitely without cash as long as we stay here. We don't even have to buy gasoline as we've rounded up three riding horses. We started out in the Ford the other day calling on such of the kin as we thought might have horses to lend and were very lucky, coming home with two horses, saddled and bridled. Allen drove and Cath[2] and I rode them home by the moonlight. It was grand. I'd forgotten how much I love to ride. Two of the horses are ponies (Not colts, darling) and saddle beautifully and the third is an aged saddle mare who moves always as if she were heading a parade.

Life here is that rich and strange that I've hardly got settled to work as yet but I have my papers out, as K. A. is always saying, and I have hopes. Meanwhile I am distributing the manure over the asparagus bed. Nick[3] just dumped it down in his usual fashion. We have a pet lamb that eats out of a bottle. His name is Micajah. He sleeps in a hen nest at night and often trots into Miss Carrie's bedroom, which enrages her.[4]

Andrew has been begging us to go to Alabama and stay with him and his father[5] until our house is vacant in October. But my grandmother insists that she may not be here next winter and we decided to stay here though I think we are rather a trial to the old lady. There really isn't enough room as the old lady insists on keeping her summer bedroom and her winter bedroom inviolate though she can only stay in one at [a] time. It has been decided that Uncle Doc,[6] the aged drunkard who sort of lives around with us is the one to go and I of course had the job of telling him. He resists the idea and in an effort to prove that he is indispensable hammers madly day and night upholstering old sofas and chairs. He also plunks his guitar and croons of evenings. We are summoned to breakfast by eight loud twangs on the guitar signifying eight o'clock. Thank God, we have a cook or it would all be too much. A fine country nigger. We pay her three dollars a month! She asked me as a special favor if she could come in the room and watch me typewrite some day! I sternly said I'd have to think about it. It is all quite mad but it has always been that way here and I suppose we'll be able to settle down to work soon. Allen has started, in fact.

I wish now that we had telegraphed the Atlantic that we thought Ford would let them have the article[7] instead of just telegraphing his address. However I'm sure it will be all right. Everything is held up now.

The party for the nuptials of K. A. and Gene[8] seems to me a work of supererogation—unless you just felt like you had to have a party. A little conviviality helps in times like these.

A funny thing happened the other day. Seward Collins, who owns The Bookman, wrote Donald Davidson[9] that he was converted to agrarianism and wanted to make The Bookman its organ. He says he will depend on the agrarian group for advice and contributions, so there is a market for us people of sound principles if Collins keeps the stand he's taken.

My neck is still slightly dislocated. The doctor on the boat says that I did not do it posing for you. He says it takes fifteen hundred pounds of weight to put a vertebra out of place and so on and says it is an alurgic [*sic*] phenomenon. I think perhaps though that you had better stick to my story. It will make a fine legend for you. Painters will be telling refractory models that Biala broke a model's neck once and thought nothing of it.

The [Phelps and Una] Putnams—we stopped a week with them in Maryland—admired the Castle of the Good King Rene no end. Such of the kin as have viewed it do not care for it at all. And they do not like that portrait of Stella's either.

I tell myself that nobody really ever starves to death but I can't help being rather worried about you all. Why doesn't Bradley[10] do something—but it's just like him to be caught without cash.

Uncle Doc in his passion to be useful, poor devil, wants to take this to the mail so I'll quit. Let me hear from you [as] soon as you can. I suppose the Lippincott advance would fix up everything if you could only get your hands on it.

Love to both of you,

c.

Merry Mont
Trenton, Kentucky

Moe's cheque has just come! In the same mail came a note from Stella saying Ford had just called up to say his cheque had come. I hope this means the financial strain is over!

1. This letter is missing.
2. Catherine Wilds, Gordon's cousin.
3. Nick Dudley, hired hand at Merry Mont.
4. That is, Gordon's grandmother.
5. Robert Logan Lytle.
6. A boarder ordinarily staying at the house of Gordon's aunt Loulie Meriwether.
7. See *CG 16*.
8. Katherine Anne Porter and Gene Pressly were married in Paris on March 18, 1933, with Ford as best man.

9. Poet and essayist; professor at Vanderbilt University and one of the group
   who championed the movement known as Regionalism.
10. William A. Bradley, Ford's agent in Paris.

CG 18. CG to JB. TLS. 2 ll. [Apr.? 1933] Merry Mont.

My poor dear Janice:

It must have been your prophetic soul that used to inveigh against
Mme Lamure's passion for the Tates. And now alas, look what has
come on you. I know how a nasty job like sending off that sweater can
weigh on the mind. It came today. A swell sweater, such a heavenly
shade of green but I am embarassed to think of their making it for me.
I have just written them a letter, in Little Rollo style,[1] so at least Mme
will absolve you of the charge of pinching it. Too bad you couldn't. It
is just your color. God knows I would have been pleased.

I am certainly thankful that you all weathered the moratorium
so well. I never was certain about the Lippincott advance, whether
it really cleared things up and kept thinking that maybe I ought to
have sent you some of the Guggenheim cheque. I delayed a day or
two and of course it vanished like mist. The creditors had been
quite complaisant till we arrived home then they burst out like a
rash.

I had been wondering whether you all weren't back at Toulon and
then somebody or other wrote that Peter Blume[2] had the place we
had in Paris which I thought must be Denfert-Rochereau. I have not
had the decency to even write the Pressleighs to congratulate them on
their marriage. But there has been so much to do here and I have been
trying to get back to my novel [*The Garden of Adonis*]. Seven chapters
done now and eight to go. And they certainly go slowly.

It must be marvellous there now. We've had a late, rainy spring.
Still the countryside is beautiful enough to make you want to stop
work. All the woods white with dogwood now. Yesterday Cath [Wilds]
and I walked to Cloverlands through the woods and found beds and
beds of wild iris.

We planted our garden the other day, with the help of four negro
men and two mules. We are going to try to raise quantities of stuff,
five long rows of onions and a lot of late potatoes to carry us through
the winter. If I could ever get that damn Benfolly on a self sustaining
basis then we could all just draw in our belts a little when one of these
crises came along. My grandmother has decided that she can't stand
Buff Orpington chickens and is switching to Plymouth Rocks. She is
going to give me all the B.O.'s when I move back to Benfolly this fall.
(I trust these chicken notes won't rouse envy in the breast of Ford.)

The American Review is now launched (successor to the Bookman). [Seward] Collins came down a week or two ago, saw and was fairly well conquered. The connection between the magazine and the agrarians is to be unofficial which is probably just as well as he is a man who is always rushing from one thing to another. He hasn't decided yet whether he will include poetry and fiction—he thinks they are hardly worthy of serious attention. I imagine he'll decide against them. There were some funny sidelights to the conference. Collins doesn't drink and we had got hold of some very good liquor to sustain ourselves during his visit. He also didn't bring any dinner clothes and all the ladies who had been invited to meet him at a formal dinner were hurriedly donning velvet jackets. They took him to Andrew Lytle's plantation in Alabama for the conference. The conferees were invigorated by one of those old fashioned Southern breakfasts, three or four kinds of meat and so on. Collins takes only weak tea for breakfast. Allen said Mr. Lytle[3] looked rather baffled when he found this out. He would have said "Certainly, just a minute" if he'd been asked for a roasted ox, but tea was too much for him. They finally found a package of jasmine tea left by Andrew's aunts in a remote cupboard.

Malcolm Cowley is thinking of coming down here for his vacation and to finish a book.[4] This house is too full already but he may stay at Cloverlands, half a mile away.

We have beer now, thank God. In Kentucky. Tennessee will have it May 1. We drive to Guthrie fourteen miles away for beer. It's pretty good beer too. The restaurateurs of Guthrie, population 1000, took in over two thousand dollars the first day, mostly from thirsty Clarksvillians. You can't imagine what a difference it makes to be able to get something decent to drink.

Do write when you have time. I think of you both so often—wish I were on the terrasse of the Villa Paul this minute.

Love and my deep sympathy about the sweater. Thank God you didn't have to pay duty on it,

as ever, c.

"Merry Mont"
Trenton, Kentucky

1. The Rollo books were a series of juvenile novels by the American educator and clergyman Jacob Abbott (1803–1879).
2. American painter. In a letter to Ezra Pound, Ford does place Peter Blume in this studio (*Pound/Ford* 123).
3. That is, Andrew Lytle's father.
4. A former expatriate himself, Cowley analyzed the postwar generation in his partly autobiographical *Exile's Return* (1934).

CG 19. TLS. 2 ll. [Early summer 1933] Merry Mont.

My dearest Ford:

I have been trying to write all morning and couldn't and found myself wishing that there was something here of yours to read for reading even a sentence of yours often arouses in me the feeling out of which writing grows. I've been reading Ezra's cantos[1] lately but I had never even glanced inside the pamphlet of testimonials[2]— the idea of testimonials to him somehow bored me even when you and Allen were talking about it last year so I didn't listen and didn't read them when they came. But the pamphlet fell out and I opened it and read your piece[3] and realized afresh that in what you write there is "beauty and emotion and excitement," even in a simple occasional piece like this one.

I thought too how some day—if you should die before I do, which is not as likely as you will say it is—I would probably set myself to write down, to get into words somehow the significance of your work. It would have to be a long way off. You can't write about a man's work, place him as we say in literature, unless you can stand away from him, can see where he fell short as well as where he excelled. And I am now and have been for some years too much under your influence, have felt too keenly the beauty and emotion and excitement of your writing to do that. I doubt if I am ever able to do it—my mind does not move that way. But I have been wishing I could communicate these things to you now, instead of to some far off shadowy public. It is—I fall back again on something somebody had said about Pound—it is "the charged word," the work that unfailingly arouses emotion. We can recognize its existence, comment on it critically but what charges the word, or why in your work the emotion is unfailingly there I can not say any more than I could lead you to the sources of the spring that gushes so profusely from the rock over there in the woods.

And you cannot really say these things so that they will be understood—it is perhaps foolish even to try.

I wonder how you both are and what you are doing. We are still at Merry Mont but expect to move back to our own house August 15. It is really beautiful over there now, larkspurs and hollyhocks and ragged robin all around the house. And a week ago the poppies were in bloom. I send you some pictures we took the other day.

Malcolm Cowley is boarding at Cloverlands, next farm to this. We try to write in the morning, go swimming in the afternoon, drink beer and talk and life is pretty dull. It rained every day for two months in the spring and now it does not rain at all—almost a month's drouth already. I had a wonderful garden, the first good garden I ever had in my life, but it is slowly drying up.

Allen is still following the plan you suggested to him for his book.[4] He has written the foreword and a magnificent long first chapter, the best piece of prose he has ever done I believe. But it is a tremendous task he's set himself, almost like writing six novels in one and he is handicapped all along by never having quite enough documentary material at hand.

Nancy returned from her sojourn in Chattanooga twenty pounds overweight, with a perfect East Tennessee accent—she asks frequently for "aahce cream." She has been listening to the radio a lot and has a repertoire of songs calculated to give a parent considerable pause. "You go home and pack your panties, I'll go home and pack my scanties and we'll shuffle off to Buffalo" is her great favorite.

Malcolm has brought all sorts of strange tales of what our friends in New York are doing but they are all doing just what I thought they would be doing when I stopped to think about it so there is no need to rehearse the stories.

Josie Herbst in spite of not knowing how to write a decent sentence, has written a fine book about reconstruction times in Georgia.[5] I have not heard one word from Katherine Anne since we left Paris. I trust she and Gene are none the less happy now they're married.

Love to Janice. I hope you have a good summer—and that your aubergines, tomatoes, and all the other things flourish,

As ever,
C.

"Merry Mont"
Trenton, Kentucky till August 15.

1. *A Draft of XXX Cantos* (1933).
2. *The Cantos of Ezra Pound: Some Testimonies* (1933).
3. "From Ford Madox Ford."
4. The novel *Ancestors in Exile*, never completed in its projected form; *The Fathers* was a reworking of Tate's idea of a family novel. Tate apparently changed the title of the book he was working on to *The Fathers* some time in 1933; cf. *CG 20*.
5. Josephine Herbst's novel *Pity Is Not Enough* was published in 1933.

FMF 8. **TLS. 3 ll. Sept. 11, 1933. Toulon.**

Toulon

11.9.33

Dearest Caroline:

I ought to have written to you long [ago]—though "ought" with its collocation of painful duty is not the right word for, once I get started it is pleasure enough. The difficulty is really in the starting. At any rate with me it is almost a necessity to have some event or mood out of the common run to start one. I really believe I write, hardened though I may seem, with as much difficulty as any schoolboy who follows his pen round his mouth with his tongue—I don't mean merely letters, I mean everything—and the condition grows. I used to write French with greater fluency than English but lately I have been writing articles and letters in French and found them as difficult as English. I don't suppose it means that I am losing fluency: merely that, as my time on earth may be presumed to be shortening, I am more and more determined to express exactly what I mean. Still I manage to turn out pretty regularly my thousand words a day at the story of Henry Martin[1] who is now really getting it in the neck.

It isn't however any special event or mood that makes me now take up, as you might say, my pen. Things go on here like a tale that is told. The drought destroyed everything in the garden except for the semi-tropical things like melons and pimento. Even the corn felt the drought. We went away for about ten days to Juan les Pins, leaving a man to water and of course he did no watering so when we got back all the strawberries and all the string beans and peas and things of a northern complexion were as dry as paper. From the middle of March till the end of September we had not a drop of rain and water in the pipes only twice a week for an uncertain hour at a time. Now however we have had two or three splendid storms and have just put in cabbages, cauliflowers, leeks, celery and sown carrots, turnips spinach and the more homespun northern things. There has been too much water for the celery and leeks which have developed rust and there are caterpillars in millions on the cabbages which look like fishing nets. Still there you are—the short and simple annals of the damn poor.

Ray Long and [Richard R.] Smith fell down on me in the spring and I transferred to Lippincott's who seem amiable but only pay me half what L & S did—and that again has to be halved because of the fall in the dollar. They are just publishing IT WAS THE NIGHTINGALE and seem rather pleased with it. So perhaps I have found my earthly home. As H[enry]. J[ames]. used to say—it would be nice to find one's final publisher but it would be rather like going into an almshouse! I don't think I should much mind that if one had a nice copper kettle on the hob and you to bring me packets of snuff—and it may well come to that yet.

We seem to have seen a lot of people this summer but I do not much remember whom. The Bogan-Holden[2] was with us for two or three days and then went to Mme Lamure's for some more. The [Cecil and Margaret] Wright's have taken up their abode in the Villa Florida, below the garden. They had a lot of people too and our garden path became an almost too boisterous high way. However they are away now. She had to have an operation in Town— meaning London—and he is in attendance on his father's death bed. The Sawyer's[3] have opened a boarding house in Juan les Pins— it was with them that we were staying, Mrs Sawyer developing on acquaintance to be a most charming person and a very good painter. They had to open the boarding house because their tenant ran away leaving them with so many debts that they had to pay for him that they could see no other way to make anything out of their house. I don't know how the experiment has succeeded. Julie is in London with her mother who fled before the rising franc—or the falling pound. I don't like it much—for I should have preferred Julie never to learn English and certainly not to go to an English school and become the usual English hobbledehoy.

Janice's brother Jack [Tworkov] was with us for a couple of the sum- mer months. He found France effete, used up and militarist but today we had a letter from him to say that he was a changed man and home- sick for Päris. Incidentally he has told their parents of Janice's mar- riage to me—a fact that she had concealed from them because she was afraid that they would commit suicide at the idea that she had married a Gentile. However, as my Great Aunt, Pet Marjorie's poem says they both were more than usual calm and never said a single darm—which is great relief to Janice, and indeed to myself. And that— as Bon Gaultier[4] says—is all my tale: sirs, I hope 'tis new t'ye: here's your ferry coot health: and tamn the whisky duty ... You will say I am getting into my dotage with all these quotations. I forgot to say that Janice and I have been working very hard for some months, she earn- ing golden opinions and selling a picture or two which is why we are not stark naked. As for myself modesty forbids my saying what I think about my novel—but the RASH ACT has made rather a stir in London and my star there seems to be rising again—which you might call calling the Old World in to redress the balance of the old [new]; for L[ong] & S[mith] declared themselves bankrupt on the day after its publication in New York and it sold practically nothing, which is a pity as it was my best book—more, that is to say, like what I really want to write than anything I have yet done. So that's that.

I should probably have written to you much sooner but for your letter [CG 19] about my work. Not that I wasn't touched and pleased and covered with blushes. But I never do know what to do with praise: If I say: "Yes, pretty good!" it seems fatuous and if I say "Pretty damn bad" it is almost worse. And I was feeling as a matter of fact rather bad about most of my old work and had not begun the new book—but you know that I must have been pleased—and how much pleased.

And what are you doing? I hope daily that the post will bring me your novel [*The Garden of Adonis*] or at least the manuscript of it. But it does not come. It seems ages since you left these shores—but of course ten months is but a day in the courts of the Novel. Still it is nearly time.

And Allen's Ancestors? Someone—I don't know who, perhaps Louise Bogan, said they had gone to the publisher and would appear about now. I felt dubious but I hoped. Did PENHALLY ever find a London publisher?[5] I told Cape to send it back to me but the fool said it had gone back to you and I gave up butting in because I did not know what you wanted.

Katherine Anne seems to be really working hard. We hear from them occasionally. They are feeling pretty good just now because Gene is being paid in dollars of frs twenty five apiece and in addition he has had a rise. But they had a pretty thin time until lately.

Well, now we jog and stagger through the autumn. It is just about a year since we came back from Germany with the Strasburg paté and just about two since I was setting out from New York to go down to you. But no, three!!!! Truly the waters flow under the bridge and the little stones find their places as says a Spanish proverb of my own invention.

Nancy, I suppose, is now a young woman—and you are all back in Benfolly. At any rate I like to think so because your grandmother's seems to me a rather gloomy place in which to winter.

I'm afraid there is no chance of our getting to Paris this year on account of what is called the *res angusta domi*[6]—which means inflation. So we shall just have to sit here and eat rabbits of which we have raised a tribe this year. By the bye we have to announce the wedding of Mr Richard Chipper to Miss Liza of Lambeth, a most outrageous Cockney who literally hen-pecks him all day long and half the night whilst he behaves like a bewildered Marquis amongst canaries.—I meant to conclude the first sentence of this paragraph with the words—"and still less to New York." But in dreams I behold Clarksville.

So may all nice things be yours

Yr

F.M.F.

P.S. Does attached letter say anything to you? The young fellow appears to belong to the Junior Journalist's club of Nashville. Also is there anywhere in your neighbourhood any sort of dealer in old books and manuscripts? I want to sell the ms of IT WAS THE NIGHTINGALE and used to sell things through Goldsmith of Lexington Avenue.[7] But he seems to have disappeared. At any rate I can get no answer to my letters. A fellow called Howe of Cincinnatti[8] used to collect me, but I feel a certain shyness about approaching him direct and I don't like to send the Ms to just any dealer. Could I perhaps mail the ms to you and would you hold it whilst the putative dealer proposed the deal to the Cincinnatian? If it *did* come off we might still drink to you after midnight mass in St Etienne du Mont.

Dear Caroline—

I don't know on what fact Ford bases his statement as to Mr. Howe being a Cincinnatian, but it doesn't matter. And he slurs over the fact that we want to know if you know anything about Mr Mc Lean.[9] He sounds mad but if there were anything in it it might keep the wolf from all our hearthstones. I didn't write because I was waiting for Ford to do so. We're all right except for the Ford ills but that's no news. But I'm hoping to win the French lottery tho I'm still debating whether it's wise to cast that 100 frs. on the waters. K.A. is also hoping to win it. I'd be just as pleased as I'd make her buy some pictures at a good stiff price. I did a life size figure portrait of Ford in a desk chair which might impress even Allen. If I ever get a photograph of it I'll send it to you. It's so startlingly real that having left Ford in the garden, it's startling every now & then to catch a glimpse of it thru the door. With love to you & Allen

Janice

Isn't there a literary society might like to buy it?[10]

1. *Henry for Hugh* (1934).
2. The poet Louise Bogan and her husband Raymond Holden, poet and novelist.
3. Warren Sawyer, presumably a photographer by profession, and his wife; cf. *FMF* 9.
4. Pseudonym for the Scottish poet and biographer Sir Theodore Martin (1816–1909), author of humorous verse and prose.
5. The London publisher Lovat Dickson brought out *Penhally*.
6. Ford's Latin phrase might be translated as "straitened circumstances at home."
7. Alfred Goldsmith, book dealer.
8. W. T. H. Howe of the American Book Co. in Cincinnati.
9. Vance McLean, magazine editor.

10. This letter was published (with omissions) in *Letters of Ford Madox Ford*, ed. Richard M. Ludwig (Princeton: Princeton Univ. Press, 1965), 227–29.

CG 20. TL. 3 ll. [Oct. 1933] Benfolly.

Dearest Ford:

Your letter has just come and I am so happy to hear from you all. I have been wondering so how things were going and yesterday setting out some winter honeysuckle in a driving rain I bethought that you too would be gardening fiercely at this time of year.

Mr. Vance McLean's letter sounds a little mad, don't you think? Of course many editors of magazines are both mad and illiterate— I suppose the point is whether he has any money. I never heard of him—I don't know whether that means anything or not. I'll write him a letter and ask if he's in the market for non-Scandinavian fiction and see what that brings forth.

About the manuscript:[1] why couldn't Allen or I act as your agent and state that we have a manuscript of yours we are willing to sell. If you'll send some addresses to write to I'll attend to it right away.

I'm so glad about Janice's pictures. Do send us a photograph of the portrait[2] as soon as you can. I've moved the Good King Rene all over the house. It's finally ended up on the north wall of the dining room and Julie high up between the two west windows.

We are back at Benfolly dug in for the winter. My aunt [Loulie Meriwether] has come to stay with us awhile and insists on doing all the housekeeping which leaves me perfectly free to write, only I was never in a worse state for writing in my life. I have had to abandon my novel [*The Garden of Adonis*] temporarily and am now engaged in writing my father's autobiography.[3] I am calling it—it is in the guise of fiction—The Life and Passion of Alexander Maury and it tells about his humble origins and struggles from the time he really knew nothing much except Sir Izaak Walton's directions for scouring worms[4] to the time when he became a great man, the morning, that is, on the Caney Fork river when he really felt there was nobody could cast any better than he did. It is pleasant work, rather like knitting. Still, having the story and the style to a large extent off my time I'm able to make some experiments in timing. I'm trying to make it read as fast as a novel. Scribner's haven't given me a contract on it yet but talk as though they may. Anyhow I had to do something.

We are broker than ever. I do not think my aunt will last long as housekeeper. She has always been poor but she had never experienced our hand to mouth, or meal to meal kind and it makes her rather nervous. I am trying to get as much work as possible done while she's here.

We had wonderful crops this year. We have sowed crimson clover in the bottom, are going to turn it under and expect to have extraordinary corn next year as a result.

My God, I just got around to looking at the back of the enclosed envelope. 810 Broadway is the address of the Methodist Publishing House in Nashville. This young man must have been working there—it is an enormous concern. John Ransom discovered a poet there the other day—he uses such exotic words that I couldn't understand a word of his poetry—but his name is Ed Frost so this can't be he.

I have not heard a word from the Porter-Pressleighs since I left Paris. But then I'm ashamed to say that I haven't written them a word either.

Eliot published my story, "Old Red," in the Criterion this month. I sent Penhally to Faber and Gwyer via an agent—I thought it was time to quit bothering my friends about it—but haven't heard from them yet.

Allen has NOT finished The Fathers [i.e., *Ancestors in Exile*].

Leonie Adams is married, to a man some people call "Wild Bill Troy."[5] I met him once at a tea party. He was very serious. He used to contribute to a magazine Munson[6] had called "The Figure in the Carpet."

Malcolm Cowley spent the summer at Cloverlands, writing a book [*Exile's Return*] about the ideas of young men of his generation. Stark Young[7] came by on his way to Texas not long ago. We haven't seen anybody else from New York. We go to Nashville occasionally to a football game or a meeting of the Agrarians who are getting out a new symposium.[8] But most of the time we stay right here. Neither of us has got much work done this summer but we keep hoping we will.

I raised a flock of twenty three beautiful golden Buff Orpingtons this summer. You should see them. I now have forty chickens—the tenant on the place raised me some more during my absence. I am having coops built and expect to raise lots of chickens in the spring—this will make you jealous. We also have a marvellous Jersey cow but do not get any milk on account of Uncle Doc who has come to live with us. The cow was giving three gallons of milk before he began milking her—she now gives one. We are always thinking that we will get up early and catch Uncle Doc milking the cow—he sells the first, secret milking to the filling station people—but we never do so we always have something to be excited about. My aunt, a practical woman, suggests that we buy our eggs and milk from Uncle Doc and we are going to do it as soon as we get enough money but at present we just have to go without the milk and eggs.

Much love to you both. I would like to be at the Villa Paul today. Sunday:

I wrote to Mr. McLean and this is the somewhat goofy answer I got back. Shall I tell him that I'm acting as your agent and that you are always paid in advance or just let him alone?

1. Of Ford's *It Was the Nightingale*.
2. Biala's portrait of Ford.
3. *Aleck Maury, Sportsman* (1934), based on James Maury Morris Gordon's life, has a first-person narrator.
4. *The Compleat Angler* (1653) by Izaak Walton (1593–1683).
5. William Troy, writer; took part in a round table discussion at Olivet in 1938 together with Ford, Léonie Adams, and Katherine Anne Porter.
6. Gorham B. Munson, co-editor of the magazine *Secession* (1922–24).
7. Author of the best seller *So Red the Rose* (1934), set in Mississippi during the Civil War.
8. *Who Owns America?* (1936).

FMF 9. TLS. 2 ll. Nov. 22, 1933. Toulon.

Toulon

22 Nov 33

Dearest Caroline;

I am glad that at least you have luck with your hens. We have never had sufficient capital to replace the ones that disappeared[1] so now we are reduced to two barren doe rabbits; two canaries and the black and white cat with such other dogs and cats as choose to come in—and they are many and a great nuisance. However I see that Allen has got a poetry prize[2] which is better than nothing. On the other hand Janice has dropped a hundred francs on the National Lottery which we had hoped would land us this morning frs 5,000,000 and it has rained incessantly for the last month though today again we had the sunny south in all its glory, so may be the rainy season is over.

Everybody here is ruined or has returned to New York or both so we sit almost alone on our hilltop except that Mr Aldous Huxley[3] has asked to be allowed to call. Stella on the other hand is covering the walls of London with miles of portraits of K.C.'s[4] and Generals.

With regard to Uncle Doc and cow and eggs: if you rub the udders of the cow with powdered alum last thing at night his clients will cease purchasing their milk from him and if with sympathetic ink you write on a few eggs "Uncle Doc stole me" and deposit them in the nests he will probably leave the eggs alone very shortly because the legend will appear as soon as they are put into water to boil. *Very* old eggs are suitable for this.

Why did you have to abandon your novel [*The Garden of Adonis*]? But I daresay you will make something nice out of your father. I go on slogging away at my novel [*Henry for Hugh*] and suppose it will be done some day though it gets longer and longer. IT WAS THE NIGHT-INGALE seems to be getting a good press in New York. If you don't know—and how should you?—it is the continuation of RETURN TO YESTERDAY—up to 1925. It was self sacrificingly typed out by Gene Pressly who went blind over it and now has to wear strong spectacles! If you could sell the ms it would be grand. But can you? I know of nobody who would buy it but Mr Howe of Cincinnati and all I know of him is that he has bought all the other ms. I ever sold. It is the complete ms; in extremely tiny and impressive hand; bound in green shagreen and boxed—but unless you know somebody in Cin. who could give you Howe's address I don't see what you could do about it. I don't suppose Vanderbilt University would want it.

Eliot's printing of OLD RED may yet save his soul alive—or at least in the state of suspended animation that is its peculiar pre-rogative. I hope he paid decently for it.

As for Maclean[5]—I leave it to you, partner. Perhaps you may hear some more of him. I don't, I mean, want to turn down a good venture—at the same time I should not like to find myself printed along W. L. Phelps[6] or writers for Hearst.

Yes, it is a pity that you are not at the Villa Paul today. For yesterday I can't say, since it was one continuous thunderstorm from midnight to midnight. But today is divine and now I suppose we are in for clear cold weather till next spring.

I hope Nancy is enjoying herself and is enjoyable to you. Julie is at school in London in one of those highbrow crank schools—that I do not like at all. Janice is now thirsting to take up the pen.

Yr

FMF

; . . . . Janice speaking in continuation of ms on page 1.
Dearest Caroline

Don't pay too much attention to what Ford says about the mss. There probably are other people who'd buy it if they could be found. Would it be a great trouble to get hold of a Cincinnatti telephone book and see if you could find that gent? And offer him the ms. We are like the French Government's budget, there's enough to last us till January. After that we shall have to inflate—on air! You're an angel to suggest going to the trouble.

I'm in mourning over the 5,000,000 frs I didn't win. But I must admit I'd have been very astonished if I had. The first drawing was won by a hairdresser in Tarascon—whom Ford knows—he's going to have a free bullfight every Xmas. The second by a coal-man in Avignon and he, so far, isn't proposing to do anything philanthropic. So the High Gods do not care for us artists. Damn the High Gods!

The Pressly Porters on the other hand are living on the gold $ and K.A. is adored by her publisher, Mr [Donald] Brace who came specially from New York last week to say [so?]. So, to some, publishers are better than Gods. Also she's really working.

The [Cecil and Margaret] Wrights have gone to London and I've a feeling they'll stay there, living there being so cheap. Toulon this year has become impossible from the point of view of prices. The town is spreading in all directions and is growing so prosperous that poor people will have to leave it. I wish to God we could. We shall never survive if we have to pay these prices much longer. It was bad enough when the dollar was worth something but now one pays out three days' work to have a jacket lined. That happened to me the other day and it has really struck terror into me.

However, today I've had [a] letter from Mr Jefferson Jones of Lippincotts'—he writes to me in preference to Ford or [William A.] Bradley—to say that they're re-printing IT WAS THE NIGHTINGALE and that it has had a splendid press and that it's an honour to publish for Ford. I suppose he'll be coming from Philadelphia next—to see *me* especially as he says the cover also is very much praised.

Love to you & Allen

Janice

Love & Merry Xtmas—in
case this takes so long—to
all at Benfolly from us both. [FMF]
Warren Sawyer is going to take some photographs of my pictures. If any come out I'll send you one of Ford & yourselves.

---

1. See *CG 10*.
2. Midland Author's Prize from the magazine *Poetry*.
3. English satirist, who in his novel *Brave New World* (1932) offered a scathing critique of modern science.
4. Knight Commanders.
5. See *FMF 8* and *CG 20*.
6. William Lyon Phelps, author of the long-lasting column "As I Like It" in *Scribner's* magazine.

CG 21. TLS. 1 l. [Dec. 1933] [Benfolly]

Dearest Ford and Janice:

I was so glad to get your letter. The pictures are grand, particularly the table scene. You both look very gay. I trust that this festive season finds you even gayer—I just this morning waked up to the fact that Christmas is inevitably coming—I have been working like the devil trying to get a section of my manuscript[1] off to Perkins by the end of the month and hadn't realized it was on the way.

It finds us as always broke. Our affairs always seem to be in a worse shape as the year ravels itself out. However we already begin to feel a little festive, the Christmas turkey, raised painstakingly by my grandmother, being already penned under the lattice. I wish you all were here!

Red Warren and Cinina arrive Saturday to spend the whole Christmas with us and Manny[2] has already come. Andrew is coming up from Alabama bringing a brace of guineas, some hog killing and a gallon of sorghum. He will be a very welcome guest. I see all these people coming and wonder how in the devil we will feed them all. (At this moment we haven't even money to buy a stamp for this letter but God doubtless will provide.)

Last night we celebrated the beginning of the season by charades. I am afraid Nancy will get a taste for the stage. She was allowed to stay up and did very well in several roles, specially as Lady Godiva. She also enacted the part of the infant Ford at the bier of his aunt [Christina] Rossetti and the infant Pope being taken to call upon Dryden in a tavern. (The first part of Rossetti we considered very good: Hemingway in a high hat calling upon Gertrude Stein who explained to him her motto of A Rose Is A Rose Is A Rose.) Manson[3] acted the part of a mad ox very creditably in your name charade and Allen wearing a battered gray hat with a pillow stuffed in his front and walking with a slight limp made us all quite homesick to see you in the cafe scene.

With these innocent diversions we spend our nights and keep trying to work by day. I have hopes of finishing my book but hardly in time for spring publication.

I have written to Allen's brother's secretary asking her to try to find Mr. Howe's name[4] in the telephone directory but haven't got it yet. I will write to Mr. [Vance] McLean and tell him that you will write an article if paid in advance according to your usual custom.

It has rained four days and four nights. The cistern is full for the first time since we've been here. All the guests can have hot baths, even if they don't eat.

Sally came a week ago and departed yesterday for Rochester. She left the enclosed note to be forwarded to Cecil Wright if you know his address. Try to get it to him if you can. She took some drawings of his and I believe has some money from their sale for him.

I wish I could see you both and that we could spend Christmas together. Love and the best wishes for the year,

As ever,

C.

(over)

I've just got Howe's address: W. T. H. Howe of The American Book Co. Cincinnati. I've written him.

1. Of *Aleck Maury, Sportsman.*
2. Marion Meriwether, Gordon's cousin.
3. Manson Radford, Gordon's cousin.
4. See *FMF 8.*

1934–1935

CG *22*. TL. 2 ll. [Late Sept. 1934] Memphis.

My dearest Ford and Janice:

About a month ago I was coming through Memphis on my way back to Benfolly after a week in New Orleans and was put to sleep on the second floor of a suburban bungalow on Avalon street. It was too hot to sleep so I read P. G. Wodehouse[1] most of the night and at intervals reflected that while I have had a rather trying life I had escaped having to live in such a house. We are now installed in just such a bungalow—Allen calls it "The Hamburger House" and it does closely resemble a hamburger, on the outside at least. Inside there is room to turn around in and there is even a scrap of a back yard where I've planted flags from Benfolly. We got here rather suddenly. Red was offered a job teaching at Southwestern college here. He got a better offer and turned this one over to Allen. I don't think Allen can last more than a year but we had to do something. No money whatever coming in and some pretty pressing debts. Of course if it takes all the salary to live on we'll be worse off than we were. Still we thought we'd try it.

It has been so long since I've had any news of you all. I hope there's good news but that you've been too busy to write it. I don't even know just where you are now but imagine you, anyhow, at the Villa Paul, on the terrasse in very bright sun, eating breakfast, perhaps, on a blue checked table cloth. I wrote you a letter, Ford, just after reading "It Was The Nightingale" but fell into such despondency on contemplating my own paragraphs after yours that the letter got mixed up in my welter of manuscript and never again came to light. Other people— this was at Benfolly—have been reading The Nightingale too. In fact the other night when amid much gin drinking and clatter there was talk about somebody's writing Allen suddenly staggered to a book case, dragged down It Was The Nightingale, picked a passage at random and read it with such a remarkable effect—it was as if you were in the room. The thing that particularly impressed me about the book was the ease with which you reached out and dragged anything you wanted into your own private whirlpool—I had been all winter discarding a lot of good material because I couldn't handle it. I have heard, I don't remember how, that you are going to write a book on Provence. I have been very much excited by the idea. It seems to me that it might be the most beautiful book you have ever written. Indeed I feel that it will. Please tell me that you are going to write such a book.

My own book was finished some weeks ago and is on the press now. It had been titled, badly, I think, by Scribner's salesmen: "Aleck Maury, Sportsman." I had what I thought was a good title: "The Life and Passion of Alexander Maury." Perkins liked it too but the salesmen said it smacked of memoirs and Perkins says the salesmen's personal support is too valuable to dispense with so I let them do as they pleased about it. I believe they are going to try hard to sell the book. They have been making a good deal of stir about it before publication, showing it to influential people here and there. They are using what seems an odd technique to me; starting it out as purely a sportsman's book and trying to work from this special sale into a wider one. They say the same technique was used with Sassoon's Fox Hunting Man's.[2] It seems like putting the cart before the horse to me.

We hated terribly to leave Benfolly just at this, the best time of the year. We had quite a round of company just before we left: Herbert Agar and his wife,[3] Virginia Moore, Red and Cinina and so on. Unfortunately we made merry up to the last minute and got off in quite a daze, leaving behind most of the important things. But it's only two hundred miles and we are going back in October to get Allen's winter hat and the electric iron and sell the corn crop. Corn is higher than a cat's back this year with cattle starving all over the country from the drouth and we hope to get a good price. We had a good crop, good hay crop too, but no garden whatever. I hated so to leave my chickens. I had about thirty, after eating fried chicken all summer. And Manson Radford, the young poet who lived in the cabin last winter, had raised a flock of very handsome black Minorcas and had given them to me when he had to go away. Do you know the breed? They are large and their feathers have the most beautiful blue-green sheen, almost like a parrot's.

We couldn't rent the house, even for a song, so we moved the Sanctified One[4] and his five children into the kitchen and the servant's room, locking them off from the plumbing which they would certainly demolish.

I had a letter from Katherine Anne not long ago. She said they might come to America this fall, in November, on Gene's long leave. I do so hope they do, though whether they'll get as far south as Memphis God knows. Memphis is pretty deadly. The niggers here are wonderful, though and that's a help. The Hamburger house is on a hideous street but we [live] right beside a beautiful park and in the park is the "third largest free zoo in the world." I sit on a bench and watch the seals—they are the only ones who seem not to mind their captivity though it may be nervousness that makes them play so frantically. There is a black panther that reminds me very much of Shalamis.[5] It is too sad the way his eye lights up as he gazes past you and sees a bird on a bough.

Please write and tell me where you are and how and what you'll be doing this year and what Janice has been painting. If Aleck Maury should make any money I've promised myself a Biala but how can a book called "Aleck Maury, Sportsman" sell? Stark Young's book, "So Red The Rose" is selling like hot cakes. I believe it is the rather sentimental title. My book is dedicated to you. I'm a little sorry now because you will not enjoy reading it. It marches but is flimsy in spots and you will see how I could have made a really good book out of it if I hadn't been so harried. I wrote it in eight months, on five coca colas a day. Wonderful the effect Coca Cola has on the imagination but alas, it is bad for the figure. I took on fifteen pounds in three months.

Please write and much, much love to you both,

Always,

2374 Forrest Avenue

1. English writer (1881–1975) whose humorous stories about upper-class Bertie Wooster and his valet, Jeeves, have delighted numerous readers.
2. Siegfried Sassoon, *Memoirs of a Fox-hunting Man* (1928).
3. Historian and critic, co-editor (with Allen Tate) of *Who Owns America*; his wife, Eleanor, was a writer.
4. The tenant Mr. Norman was a member of a fundamentalist sect.
5. Shalammis, Biala's cat.

FMF *10*. TLS. 1 l. Oct. 12, 1934. Toulon.

> Janice says we were having breakfast
> on the terrace when your letter came.
> Also that she included Nancy in her dream.

12/10/34

Dearest Caroline;

This morning Janice said when we woke that she had dreamt that Allen had a professorial job and that you had left Benfolly. So, says I, I really must write that dedication. I got up and came to this machine and wrote the attached slip.[1] Immediately afterwards your letter came. The coincidence is not so extraordinary because you have both been in our minds a good deal lately whilst we debated whether we should go from Bordeaux to Norfolk Va. and so northwards via you or go straight to N.Y. and try to go back by Norfolk and you. I think we should have decided to go by Norfolk and drop in on you if we had been certain that you were at Benfolly; as it is we are going to take the Koenigstein on today week from Antwerp and shall arrive in N.Y. on the 1st of November being the feast of All Saints. What will happen to us then All the Saints only know for we shall arrive penniless and with only very slim prospects; but perhaps the SS. will provide, so pray for us on Halloween and, if it is not too distasteful put a candle before the image of Mary Star of the Sea.

Our going to New York is not as lunatic a proceeding as it sounds; indeed we are practically coerced into it by various stresses and Janice wants to see her parents and so on. But we feel a little tragic; the garden has never been so gorgeous as this year; the weather is still nearly tropical and infinitely benign with amazing sunsets over the Rade and the hills; if we could have stayed here it would have been in comparative—if only very comparative—ease such as we have never before known; for never yet have we been able to see a whole eighteen months ahead, that being by the cost of the voyage reduced to about a fortnight. But the die is cast, the reservations made and this time next week we shall be sailing down the Maas or the Scheldt or whatever that Batavian estuary is called. It's queer that it was from Antwerp that Janice first set sail from Europe.[2] But the Line is the cheapest we could find. The [Walter and Lillian] Lowenfels' are sailing with us—with twins and a maid. He has given up the unequal literary struggle and is taking a job in N.Y.

I thought I would startle you with this news before expressing startlement at yours—because that we should be glad that you should be casé'd[3] if only for a time. Let me first express then gratification at the dedification[4]—horrible assonance—of your novel and excitement at the thought of reading it. Pray send us a copy c/o Dr [Michael] Lake, 50 West Twelfth Street so that immediately after arrival Janice and I may fight over who is to read it first. It must be an immense relief to have got it off. All my congratulations . . . and prayers for its success.

As for us, in this twelvemonth we have been three months in London, three in Paris, then a day or two each in the English country, Paris again, Dijon, Orange, Tarascon, Avignon, Nîmes for a magnificent bull-fight, just across the Italian border, Monte Carlo, Nice and so here. Here Janice has illustrated and I have written my book about Provence.[5] Lippincotts express themselves "enchanted" with the book and "delighted" with the illustrations—so whether it is good or bad you may guess for yourselves.

At any rate it is about everything under the sun from Cézanne[6] to the Cockney accent and dialect and the sunlight itself and the Crusades against the Albigenses[7] and Cato's love for and methods of cooking cabbages[8] and the mises à mort.[9] As for that last Janice made some magnificent drawings in the arena at Nîmes whilst Lalanda and Chicuelo were actually working their bulls—and I dismiss the question of the morality of the *corrida* by saying that I like to go occasionally to a bullfight so I go occasionally to a bullfight and that's that. I thought when I had finished the book that it was the best book I had ever written and I don't know that I don't still think that. You see for the last few years I have been trying to raise the "serious" book to the level of the novel by writing it with as much passion and similar technique. And I don't know that I have not succeeded—and Janice's drawings fit the text as caviare improves and makes a Trinity—three in One and one in three—of lemon juice and hashed onions. I want to call the book ALL EVIL COMES FROM THE NORTH which is appropriate for a book dedicated to youall; Janice wants to call it FROM THE COURTS OF LOVE and I suppose Lippincotts will call it something idiotic in the end. And as it's their job I shall let them have their way. I have written so many books with perfect titles and they have not sold that I have decided to let L's try idiotic titles like HUGH FOR HENRY[10]—which book I suppose you will by now be reading. It is not perhaps too bad but I have rather lost interest in it.

As for the dedications let us stick to our guns and if people say it looks like "YouscratchmybackIscratchyours," why let 'em.

I've got to close because Pat[11] is waiting to take it to the post. All good wishes for the nonce and the rest of our news à tantôt.

Always

Yr

F.M.F.

lu et apprové

Biala (Janice)

1. Ford dedicated his book *Provence* (1935) to the Tates; see the introduction, XXVI. The "attached slip" is among the Ford Madox Ford material at Princeton University Library.
2. See the introduction, XXI.
3. French *caser:* "provide for."

4. Gordon dedicated *Aleck Maury, Sportsman* (1934) to Ford.
5. *Provence*, with illustrations by Biala, was published by Lippincott in 1935.
6. The painter Paul Cézanne (1839–1906) found his greatest inspiration in his hometown, Aix-en-Provence.
7. A religious sect that was suppressed for heresy in the middle of the thirteenth century.
8. Marcus Porcius Cato (234–149 B.C.), Roman statesman; his ideal was the simplicity of a mainly agricultural state.
9. A French bullfighting term ("the kill").
10. *Henry for Hugh* was published in October 1934.
11. See *CG 9*.

CG 23. TLS. 2 ll. [Late Oct. 1934] Memphis.

I seem to have lost what little sense I had. Immediately on reading your letter I rushed to the phone and sent a cable. I misread your letter, thinking you were sailing on All Saints' and it's then you're landing in New York. Never mind. You have my greetings at this end. My dearest dears:

I could not get to work this morning for thinking that the mail might bring some news—how telepathic we are all getting!—and what news it is. You will be in New York when you get this letter! I can't yet take it in. Oh how I wish we had been at Benfolly and you could have landed at Norfolk us meeting you there and we could have had some time together there on the river in October. It will have to be enough, though, to know you're in the country. It's maddening to think we're tied up here for months.

You had better come to Benfolly after you get your New York affairs attended to and let us come visit you for week ends. Certainly you will come to Benfolly by spring time anyhow? The house is there, fairly ready for occupancy. We took away only enough stuff to furnish a small apartment. Not being able to get a paying tenant we moved our non paying tenants, the Normans, into the kitchen and servant's room. They can, however, be moved out at a moment's notice into their own cabin in the spring hollow. The other cabin—we have moved it into the locust grove and painted it white and it is really quite sweet now is also crying for occupancy. And sooner or later you must come and inhabit one or other of these houses. I will allow you a *little* time in New York beforehand, though.

Your books come so fast and furiously I cannot keep up with them. I have just finished reviewing Henry for Hugh for Scribner's.[1] I didn't know you'd written it till they sent me the copy—and now to think that the book about Provence is already written, and illustrated! I'm anxious to see Janice's illustrations. I thought the Henry for Hugh cover was swell. But the drawings at Nimes will be more exciting.

"All Evil Comes From the North" naturally rings my bell. "From The Courts Of Love" might ring more bells perhaps. And as you say Lippincott's will suit themselves. I am getting rather reconciled to the title of my own book. They have handled it on the dust cover so it reads more just "Aleck Maury," the "Sportsman" being subordinated. They are advertizing it—in the same breath with Queen Marie of Roumania,[2] Philo Vance[3] and William Lyons Phelps—as "the unsurpassed novel of the outdoors." Meanwhile I have a market with Scribner's for sporting stories. It's rather difficult as I know nothing about sports and have pumped my unfortunate father dry. I have to begin picking other people's experiences out of them now and then putting them together painfully into a sort of mosaic.

Your dedication[4] is lovely and we are very proud to have it. My own[5] is terser as I don't think you're going to like the book very much.

We are expecting the [John Peale] Bishops up from New Orleans this Saturday. They have been in America for nearly a year now, with only one French maid!

Nancy is outrageously fat and sassy, ecstatic just now over the acquisition of an Angora guinea pig. The Angora helps to disguise the ratlike quality very nicely. I had sworn I wouldn't have even a pet cockroach this year and here I am with a guinea pig.

Tell Janice she will find Primrose Ann, Blue Tato, Colonel Crockett and Tri-Couleur to welcome her at Benfolly. I still have the feeling that you'll land there. The Black Minorcas and the cow and calf also await your coming. Don't you think you will tire of city life soon?

Allen's work here is too heavy. He has no time or energy left for writing. We will stick it out nine months anyhow. We have arranged to have a hundred dollars for our debts taken out of his salary each month so by living very close to the knuckle all winter we may have our heads above water by spring. And of course I'm hoping a little that Aleck Maury may make us some money. Scribner's really are prepared to push it I hear from all quarters. I hope Janice brought my picture[6] over.

I shall go to work immediately trying to get up a lecture that will pay enough to bring you to Memphis. Unfortunately this damn Goodwyn Institute here makes up all its programs a year ahead and imports people like Ludwig Lewisohn.[7] I'll try the clubwomen but they are notoriously stingy. We'll work it somehow, though.

This letter is probably incoherent. I'm still so dazed at the thought of seeing you both again. It's heinous that you're to be in New York and we here and months may intervene before we see each other. But I *am* glad you're on this side of the water, oh so glad!

My dearest love to you both. Allen doesn't know the great news yet. Do write as soon as you get there,

Caroline

2374 Forrest Avenue

Memphis

My regards to Eileen and Micky[8] who seem like old friends. I hope they will come to Benfolly too before the year is over.

1. It has proved impossible to locate the relevant issue of Scribner's in-house review, the *Bookbuyer*.
2. Queen of Roumania 1914–27, Queen Dowager 1927–38.
3. S. S. Van Dine's fictional detective; S. S. Van Dine was the pseudonym for Willard Huntington Wright.
4. See *FMF 10*.
5. See *FMF 10*.
6. Presumably Biala's portrait of Gordon.
7. Prolific American novelist and critic.
8. Dr. Michael Lake and his wife, Eileen, friends of Ford in New York.

FMF 11. TLS. 2 ll. Nov. 9, 1934. New York.

61 FIFTH AVENUE

N.Y.C.

Lord Mayor's Day '34

Dearest Caroline;

Here we are at last settled down with electricity, gas and telephone plus electrolux refrigerator. It has been a dreadfully difficult job to get an apartment and we are really worn out with travelling miles and miles of streets and interviewing whole Gehennas of agents and janitors. However at last we found this place which sounds splendiferous and actually is convenient and cheap. We have taken it for three months and as Lippincotts are anxious that we should stay until the publication of PROVENCE—at the beginning of March—we may be here still longer. As for visiting Benfolly—I hope we may be able to, and indeed I'm determined that we will. There is a faint hope that the [Michael and Eileen] Lakes might drive us down immediately after New Year's Day, if we might bring them—but I would prefer it if we could make it after we leave here so that we could go back by Norfolk Va or Baltimore. That however would make it so late for our poor garden though actually last year we did not get there till May and yet had our best year. Let me know will you in any case if the idea of our coming with the Lakes would appeal to you. We will bring along food and things and perhaps youall could get a day or so off and we could have a nice time.

I have read ALECK MAURY gratefully as a respite from the miles and miles of janitors, piecemeal, mostly in bed, but that is not the best way to appreciate a book and I shall read it again as soon as we have finally done going to the Five & Ten. My first impression is of course that it is not exciting technically—but it *is* beautifully written—and indeed a poem, in my sense of poetry—a quiet monologue addressed to someone that one likes very much and feels completely at home with. Certainly it's not oppressively "sportif" which is all to the good.

I hear you have written a review of HUGH FOR HENRY that has brought tears to the eyes of Mr Jefferson Jones of Lippincotts'.[1] That is to say that I saw the tears in the eyes of Mr Jones when he talked of the review. He did not seem quite to believe that one of his authors could be so written about. I say every day that I must get a copy of *Scribner's* and read it but I am with[h]eld, I should think by a sort of shyness. I never can read anyone's praise of my work without a goose-fleshly sort of feeling coming over me so heaven alone knows what shall happen to me when I read you. In our wanderings we arrived at Bank Street—37 wasn't it?[2]—where the third floor is to let, but unfurnished and we had a little conversation with Mr Brooks who sent you his love. What waters have not flowed under the bridges since those days and how many little stones have found their places. . . . Otherwise I have seen noone to count much in N.Y. since we got here—certainly noone dating back to those days, unless Selma Brandt[3] does—and Cobay Gilman[4] and, I think, Mrs [Josephine] Herbst or at any rate someone like her who bowed to me from the other end of the Lafayette café. Janice is rather worn out and does not quite believe that she is living on Fifth Avenue; still she bears up.

I hope to get to some work soon: indeed if I don't we shall be on the bread-line; but my head seems filled with cotton wool—to such an extent that I have forgotten to say that we duly received your cable and letter on arrival here—which much cheered said arrival.

Goodbye, my dear. All good wishes and then many more

Yr

F.M.F.

1. See *CG 23*.
2. In 1926–27 the Tates lived at 27 Bank Street, and Ford stayed there briefly in 1927.
3. Zelma C. Brandt, literary agent.
4. See *CG 8*.

FMF *12*. ALS. 1 l. Dec. 4, 1934. New York.

4 Dec '34

Dearest Caroline:

I have now re-read *Aleck Maury* as I said I wd. &, as I expected, like it even better than I did. But the conviction grows upon me that its chief characteristic is that it's a poem rather than a novel—the tranquillity & beauty of the writing are quite outside drama wh. I suppose the novel ought to contain. And certainly you do yr. south country proud. I don't know any book that projects a country-side better. It has the quality of Turgeniev's *Sportsman's Sketches*[1]—& you cdn't have greater praise from me! To what are you going to progress now.

I find N.Y. very depressing—or at any rate I'm myself very depressed—unable to settle to my work & with a head absolutely without ideas: and steel to strike my flints with . . . and nobody here really to talk to. After that I'd better not say whom we've seen!

Why have neither you nor Allen answered my letters? But I suppose you're distracted too.

It seems as if we shd stay here till March: then if the money will run to it will pass by way of Memphis & Norfolk Va. for shipping. I hope you like being where you are.

Janice sends her love

Yrs. always

FMF.

1. *A Sportsman's Sketches* (1852; 1880) by the Russian writer Ivan S. Turgenev (1818–1883).

CG *24*. TLS. 1 l. [Dec. 1934] Memphis.

Dearest Ford:

The dedication is lovely and we're both very proud—it seems absurd that we haven't written you sooner but I've thought every day I'd get out of the morass I've been laboring in and be able to write a real letter. The morass is a short story[1] I'm trying to finish and sell to Scribner's very quickly so that we might, might just make it to New York for Christmas. It would be too grand to arrive and find you all of all people there. Quite too good to be true, I fear. I'm really not counting on it.

Are you coming New Year's as you said you might, you and the [Michael and Eileen] Lakes? I've had the feeling all along that you'd probably postpone your visit till you're ready to go home. I want to see you terribly now but if you came in the spring you might have a longer time to stay. Allen has a vacation of five days

in April. I wish we could all land at Benfolly then. We have plenty
of room for you here but it would be nice there in the spring.

Let me know if there is any chance of your coming New Year's.
Our plans—they seem rather confused—boil down to this. Allen
needs a change badly and we aren't going to stay here in Memphis
unless there's some excitement on, like your visit. If we can't raise
the money to go to N.Y. we may drive to New Orleans and spend
Christmas with the Warrens. Allen's vacation begins December 20
and ends January 3. We'll be back here January 3 in any case but
we'd come sooner if you were coming. And by the way, don't let
the prospect of our getting there influence you not to come—I
don't really see how we can make it.

I'm anxiously awaiting your book on Provence. I have no idea
how Aleck Maury is selling but not too hotly, I imagine. I fear the
title has killed it. Perhaps I should have called it "Portrait of the
Artist as An Angler" or something. But Ford, I do think it's a
novel—it's about how a man made one thing triumph over everything else in his life. Isn't that drama? I think I just didn't give him
enough complications in his life.

I've written three short stories[2] since coming to Memphis which is
quite a lot of short stories for me. It has come very near killing me.
But this is a dull place and fairly easy to work in. No, we don't like it
but we're getting a hell of a lot of debts paid off which helps some.

My love to Janice. I wonder how she finds New York after all these
years? If you all weren't there I don't believe I'd have the heart to think
even of coming. All the people we used to know there have turned
Communist and I fear they will look down on us horribly when they
see us again. Or is the Communist vogue waning in literary fashion?

Do you all have to go back to France this spring? Can't you stay
the summer at Benfolly?

Allen sends his love. This job is terrible for him. He hasn't time or
energy left even for correspondence which is why he hasn't written
you. I think it was silly of the NRA[3] or whatever it is to want ten
dollars for that quotation.

Please write me your plans right away. You seemed so near when
you first arrived in New York and now you seem so far. Effect of
Memphis on me perhaps, it's a little like living under water. Love
to Janice. I do so want to see you both. Be sure and tell the Lakes
we want them to come down too,

Love, always,

C.

2374 Forrest

1. Probably "B from Bull's Foot," rejected by two magazines and finally accepted by *Scribner's*.
2. "One More Time," "To Thy Chamber Window, Sweet," and "The Last Day in the Field."
3. Possibly National Recovery Administration. Scribner's followed the Code for Publishers in requiring payment for the lines quoted from Allen Tate's poem "The Mediterranean."

CG 25. TLS. 1 l. [Mid-Dec. 1934] Memphis.

My dearest Ford:

I was so glad to have your letter.[1]

I do not think now that we can make it to New York. Dashiell, of Scribner's Magazine,[2] has cut me from $250 to $150 on my last story though Perkins had promised me $250 for each story. This rather knocks the stuffing out of things—when things are run as we always seem to be running them on a shoe string. It was perhaps a wild plan. But wouldn't it have been fun to be there all together at Christmas! You would have had to cook our Christmas dinner for us and I would have run hither and thither to the A. and P.'s for you. Do you suppose any of us will ever have enough money to do any of the nice, simple things we like to do?

We plan now to leave here next Thursday and spend Christmas Day and a few other days at Merry Mont with my grandmother then the rest of the holidays with Red and Cinina. As long as you all are not coming we won't come back here till January third. Allen does so need a change from the college atmosphere which is pretty thick.

I had not realized really until today that Christmas was inevitably at hand. I have just been sitting here day after day writing and getting pretty tired of it at times. But day before yesterday I got the idea for my next novel, snap, like that, which is something to be thankful for. It's to be called THE CUP OF FURY. Do you like that? Jeremiah, isn't it, something about wailing at the gates and the cup of fury being lifted up.[3] It's a cup of fury for the South, of course. It would be. And it's to be a big scale, lots of people and generations. Do you think I can manage lots of people? It won't be much like Penhally. There I depended a lot on style for atmosphere; in this book the emphasis will be on characterization. I'm going to begin it right after Christmas, anyhow, sink or swim.

We have a somewhat eccentric house guest coming tomorrow: Uncle Jim Avent[4] who knows more about bird dogs than anybody in America. I rather dread him. He is a great man and knows it and moves in a sort of fabulous light. We stood in front of his cabin and he gestured over the ravine: "Gladstone has run over them fields" as one would say "Charlemagne played here as a boy." When I say Gladstone I do not refer to the premier, by the way, but to the great dog. I am thinking of writing Uncle Jim's life. He says a great many people have been wanting to write his life.

The Communist terror for me, by the way, is chiefly literary. I can't get on with the literary Communists but I think I might very well with the others. Janice's family, I believe, run to painting instead of literature.[5] My love to Janice. It's a great disappointment that we aren't to see you both though I never let myself hope very much. Well, we will count on the spring,

Dearest love, always,

C.

2374 Forrest Avenue

Good news just came with the postman. Lovat Dickson is going to publish Aleck Maury and promises $200 advance and the usual t[w]o per cent royalty up to 2500.[6] As I never seem to get above 2500 I suppose the terms don't really matter.

1. This letter is missing.
2. Alfred Dashiell, editor of *Scribner's* magazine, 1930–36.
3. Jeremiah 25:15–16: "For thus saith the Lord God of Israel unto me: Take the wine cup of this fury at my hand, and cause all the nations, to whom I send thee, to drink it./And they shall drink, and be moved, and be mad, because of the sword that I will send among them." *The Cup of Fury* was later retitled *None Shall Look Back* (1937).
4. A dog trainer.
5. Biala's brother Jack Tworkov was also a painter.
6. Ford boosted the novel by writing a blurb for it (letter to the English publisher Lovat Dickson, May 6, 1935; copy at Cornell University Library).

CG 26. CG to JB. TLS. 2 ll. [Mid-Feb. 1935] Memphis.

Dear Janice:

The drawings are *swell*.[1] I am writing Perkins in this same mail. I'm not on very good terms with him just now—I wrote, protesting against their handling of Aleck Maury the other day and he hasn't even answered the letter. They say he's so taken up with Thomas Wolfe's new book[2] these days he hardly knows what he's doing. However, let's hope he'll take time off to cast his eye on these drawings—he can't help but see how fine they are. I should think they'd be delighted to exhibit them. They'd make a swell display.

I'm glad to know you still think you can come south. Lord, I hope you make it. New York begins to seem even as far away as Toulon. And June when we hope to get free of this wretched job seems even farther. I've started half a dozen letters to you all but have been so sunk in February gloom that I never got them finished. February is the most damnable month, no matter where you are. Just now I have grippe and am writing with the typewriter perched on a pillow on my tummy. It never lasts long with me, though, and I'm hoping to be up tomorrow.

If you sail from New Orleans you must stop there with the [Manson and Rose] Radfords—the young couple who lived in our cabin last year/ We spent Christmas with them in the Sultan's House, 716 Dauphine it is. The house reminds me of 32 Vaugirard, only it has balconies with beautiful iron work around all sides of the three stories. The grillwork against the blue in the morning is so beautiful it wakes you up, even after nights of debauch. We missed you all terribly in the Christmas revels—it was all so exactly like similar times in Paris that it didn't seem right for you not to be there. I know you'll love New Orleans. The houses in the French quarter are the most beautiful I've ever seen anywhere. You really must arrange to spend a few days there. The Radfords have three enormous rooms, each one big enough for a studio on the top floor of this old house, so there'd be plenty of room for you. And they'd adore having you. But that's all in the future, of course.

I wish to God there was something I could do towards selling the book. Here's just an idea. What do you think of it? A man named Walsh[3] who used to be Scribner's advertizing man and is now on the road drops in on us every time he's in town. He's very indignant about the way they've handled Aleck Maury—the salesmen who forced me to give the book that absurd name admit now they made a mistake—and he's been doing everything he could to push it as he goes around. He wrote yesterday that a Louisville book store would be glad to display a portrait (drawing) of me that Rose Chavanne (Mrs. Radford) made if I'd send it. They'd be even gladder to have your drawings on display if you thought it worth while to send them out to the provinces. It wouldn't be worth while for just one store but I thought I might arrange to have them displayed in Nashville, Louisville and Memphis and route them from one city to another. There's an art academy here. They might be displayed there when youall come here. Let me know what you think of this so I can set the various wheels in motion.

I signed the English contract for Aleck Maury the other day— Lovat Dickson. I don't know anything about him except that Curtis Brown[4] say that he's a young and enthusiastic publisher in whom they have growing confidence. I cannot feel confidence in any publisher any more. I honestly believe Scribner's is a little worse than most. They started Stark Young's book [*So Red the Rose*] off, advertizing it as "romance of early days in Natchez, with a love interest." All it sold it has sold itself. Of course they're advertizing it like hell now it no longer needs it. Aleck Maury has sold 1300 copies. They've kept it strictly as a sporting book, heads their sporting list with General Sir Somebody's treatise on saddles and that sort of thing. My friends have raised such a row about the way they'd treated the book that I finally had the curiosity to look through two months issues of Saturday Reviews, Herald Tribs and so on and found not one single ad, and this just before Christmas.

Does Putnam's have a book store? I can't remember. If Earle Balch (he's their editor now) isn't in Europe he'd do anything we wanted done I believe. I'll make Allen write him a letter and enclose it to save time and you can use it if Scribner's doesn't come across. You could just mail him the letter and say it was Allen's suggestion and that he can communicate with you if he's interested.

I wish I could be more helpful[5] but I'm pretty dumb at this sort of thing. Congratulations on the drawings. They really are beautiful—the one with the bull fighters in different poses really knocks you over. And the entrance of the bull fighters, with that formality and yet the promise of action. And the arena itself—I'm simply mad about them.

Love to you both,

c.

Caroline

2374 Forrest Avenue

I've made the letter to Perkins as strong as I could. It goes off in this afternoon mail, with the proofs.[6]

fifty best books[7]
Mrs. Greenhead invites
send Provence to competition
Institute of Graphic Art
Grand Central Palace
Book must be there Tuesday
  Ford

---

1. Biala's illustrations in Ford's *Provence*.
2. *Of Time and the River* (1935).
3. Tom Walsh of Scribner's; he later negotiated an anthology of short stories with commentaries by Gordon and Allen Tate titled *The House of Fiction* (1950).
4. Literary and movie agents.

5. About having Biala's drawings for *Provence* displayed in a New York store.
6. Presumably of some work by Ford; cf. *CG 28*.
7. Presumably draft of a telegram sent by Ford to Gordon.

CG 27. TLS. 2 ll. [Mar. 1935] Memphis.

Dearest Ford:

It is good to have some news of you all.[1] I would have written myself before this but I have been in bed with grippe—two weeks of it. I am up now, though, and feeling fairly well. Yesterday I walked all the way to the Zoo and back—it seemed very exciting to be back in the world again.

I have not heard from Perkins in answer to my letter. But then I have not had an answer to a letter written many weeks before that. I do not know what is the matter with him—unless it is Thomas Wolfe's opus [*Of Time and the River*] coming out. I've been told that he's been dragging the words out of Wolfe one by one. And perhaps that keeps him in a strange mood—I suppose publishers are entitled to moods though it does make things inconvenient. The drawings are swell—he's a fool if he doesn't want them exhibited in the shop.

I do so hope the Provence book goes.[2] And I should think it certainly would. I'm expecting it to be your best book—and with Janice's drawings it ought to be a knock out. I can't wait to see it.

The news about the review[3] is exciting. Do let me know as soon as anything definite goes through. I will certainly round up some manuscripts for you if I can. I don't seem to meet anybody who is writing fiction but I can always put my hand on a poet or so. There's a lad at Vanderbilt named [Randall] Jarrell—Allen, [John Crowe] Ransom and all of them think he's quite extraordinary. Oh, Red Warren has one story—I hope to God he hasn't published it yet—that is really masterly: "When The Light Gets Green." It's an unfortunate title, smacking as it does of traffic. The green light is that curious light in the sky just before hail storm comes in August and kills all your tobacco. This story is perfect in the way some of Joyce's Dubliners stories are perfect.[4] He's never been able to do another one like it.

We're hoping to go to Baton Rouge in April for Red's conference[5] but don't know whether it will coincide with Allen's spring vacation from the college—he's had so much time off he rather hates to ask for any extra. Still I have an idea we'll make it, for Andrew says one must pleasure oneself as much as possible in spring. If you came here we could make the trip the rest of in [the] car which we still have or rather it still has us. (I have named it the Minotaur.) I wish you all could be persuaded not to go back to France so soon. If you're going to wait as late as June to sail can't you come to Benfolly for a while?

The gloom that has hung over the Tate household for almost two years now has lightened somewhat in the last week. Allen has suddenly begun to work again—and if a paralytic had suddenly thrown away his crutch and begun to take dance steps we couldn't be more excited, all except Nancy who takes the vagaries of the artistic temperament pretty phlegmatically.

I had a letter from Leonie Adams the other day. She spoke of seeing you all and mentioned various people that used to be in Paris—it's funny how those sort of peripheral people are always turning up wherever you go.

I think "Aleck Maury" has hit the bottom of the well you speak of—it doesn't begin to pay back the advance. But as you say there's nothing to do except go on writing other books.

It is quite definitely spring here, willows quite green and everything else budding. We had a long drive in the country this afternoon. A very strange, ragged, rather sinister looking country it is too, quite different from middle Tennessee. It is because there is no winter grass that it always looks so sodden, I think. But even the bayous are showing green—of course they have gorgeous holly trees in them green all winter but you get used to them. It will be grand if we're all able to make it to Baton Rouge. We'd have a fine time. I suppose it would be almost too much luck, though. But do let me know as soon as your plans are at all settled. By the way there is plenty of room for all of us in this hideous little house if you can only get down this far.

Much love to you both,
caroline

2374 Forrest Avenue

Memphis

last week. He has a bus ticket two yards
bund surveying the country—he expects
impressions.[6]

er that is missing.
n March 1935.
e of once more launching an international maga-
review type; as late as the spring of 1939 he was
ct (see Saunders 2: 542, 547).
es Joyce.

5. About having Biala's drawings for *Provence* displayed in a New York store.
6. Presumably of some work by Ford; cf. *CG 28*.
7. Presumably draft of a telegram sent by Ford to Gordon.

CG 27. TLS. 2 ll. [Mar. 1935] Memphis.

Dearest Ford:

It is good to have some news of you all.[1] I would have written myself before this but I have been in bed with grippe—two weeks of it. I am up now, though, and feeling fairly well. Yesterday I walked all the way to the Zoo and back—it seemed very exciting to be back in the world again.

I have not heard from Perkins in answer to my letter. But then I have not had an answer to a letter written many weeks before that. I do not know what is the matter with him—unless it is Thomas Wolfe's opus [*Of Time and the River*] coming out. I've been told that he's been dragging the words out of Wolfe one by one. And perhaps that keeps him in a strange mood—I suppose publishers are entitled to moods though it does make things inconvenient. The drawings are swell—he's a fool if he doesn't want them exhibited in the shop.

I do so hope the Provence book goes.[2] And I should think it certainly would. I'm expecting it to be your best book—and with Janice's drawings it ought to be a knock out. I can't wait to see it.

The news about the review[3] is exciting. Do let me know as soon as anything definite goes through. I will certainly round up some manuscripts for you if I can. I don't seem to meet anybody who is writing fiction but I can always put my hand on a poet or so. There's a lad at Vanderbilt named [Randall] Jarrell—Allen, [John Crowe] Ransom and all of them think he's quite extraordinary. Oh, Red Warren has one story—I hope to God he hasn't published it yet—that is really masterly: "When The Light Gets Green." It's an unfortunate title, smacking as it does of traffic. The green light is that curious light in the sky just before hail storm comes in August and kills all your tobacco. This story is perfect in the way some of Joyce's Dubliners stories are perfect.[4] He's never been able to do another one like it.

We're hoping to go to Baton Rouge in April for Red's conference[5] but don't know whether it will coincide with Allen's spring vacation from the college—he's had so much time off he rather hates to ask for any extra. Still I have an idea we'll make it, for as Andrew says one must pleasure oneself as much as possible in the spring. If you came here we could make the trip the rest of the way in [the] car which we still have or rather it still has us. (I have named it the Minotaur.) I wish you all could be persuaded not to go back to France so soon. If you're going to wait as late as June to sail can't you come to Benfolly for a while?

The gloom that has hung over the Tate household for almost two years now has lightened somewhat in the last week. Allen has suddenly begun to work again—and if a paralytic had suddenly thrown away his crutch and begun to take dance steps we couldn't be more excited, all except Nancy who takes the vagaries of the artistic temperament pretty phlegmatically.

I had a letter from Leonie Adams the other day. She spoke of seeing you all and mentioned various people that used to be in Paris—it's funny how those sort of peripheral people are always turning up wherever you go.

I think "Aleck Maury" has hit the bottom of the well you speak of—it doesn't begin to pay back the advance. But as you say there's nothing to do except go on writing other books.

It is quite definitely spring here, willows quite green and everything else budding. We had a long drive in the country this afternoon. A very strange, ragged, rather sinister looking country it is too, quite different from middle Tennessee. It is because there is no winter grass that it always looks so sodden, I think. But even the bayous are showing green—of course they have gorgeous holly trees in them green all winter but you get used to them. It will be grand if we're all able to make it to Baton Rouge. We'd have a fine time. I suppose it would be almost too much luck, though. But do let me know as soon as your plans are at all settled. By the way there is plenty of room for all of us in this hideous little house if you can only get down this far.

Much love to you both,
caroline

2374 Forrest Avenue
Memphis

Nathan Asch was here last week. He has a bus ticket two yards long on which he rides around surveying the country—he expects to make a book out of his impressions.[6]

1. Evidently refers to a letter that is missing.
2. *Provence* was published in March 1935.
3. Ford did not give up hope of once more launching an international magazine of the *transatlantic review* type; as late as the spring of 1939 he was working on such a project (see Saunders 2: 542, 547).
4. *Dubliners* (1914) by James Joyce.

5. Conference on Literature and Reading in the South and Southwest, held in Baton Rouge, Louisiana, April 10–11, 1935.
6. Nathan Asch published *The Road in Search of America* in 1937.

CG 28. TLS. 1 l. [Late Mar. 1935] Memphis.

Dearest Ford and Janice:

I had just finished a letter to you asking if you were coming to the Louisiana conference when your letter[1] arrived. This is splendid. I, too, was beginning to fear that you'd get away without our seeing you, I am so glad you are coming. We will have a grand time. The Christmas debauch was worthy to go down in history— I don't see why the April gathering shouldn't be just as successful. We must go over to New Orleans—it is only ninety miles from Baton Rouge. The [Manson and Rose] Radfords are still living on the top floor of the Sultan's house and we can all stay with them. The country is marvellous now—all the fruit trees in bloom and dogwood. It will be lovely driving down.

We hear talk already of your book [*Provence*] and are awaiting it anxiously. I am afraid you will have to submit to a tea or something here at the hands of the clubwomen, if you get here in time. And we hope you'll come a day or so beforehand if possible. There is plenty of room.

I will ask Perkins to return the proofs.[2]

I have achieved a great moral—or immoral—victory in the last few months. We were so broke that I turned my hand to writing a Saturday Evening Post story, with the aid of my trusty collaborator,[3] in which Falcon's Speed Boy by Speed Merchant out of Ensley's Flirt finds enough birds to win the National Field Trial stake thus enabling his owner to lift the mortgage from the old homestead and marry The Girl. My collaborator particularly approves of the way the "love interest" is handled—"none of this morbid, glooey love stuff" he says. The agent is also highly enthusiastic and says the Post people will take it unless they're quite mad. I don't know whether to hope they will or not. It would be hellish to have to write more of them—but it is too soon to worry about the fruits of my prostitution. As Mr. Hardy would say "you ain't ruined yet" she said.

I am so very pleased about "Provence" starting off well. It is going to be a great success—I feel it in my bones already. Well, we will all soon be drinking to its success at The Cabildo (the New Orleans equivalent of Paul's). You will both love New Orleans. You could love it for its architecture alone, and the smells. It smells very French.

I must get this in the mail. We are so very glad you're coming. Don't let anything make you change your mind. Love from all of us,

caroline

Can you tell me now whether you can stand the tea[4]—it will be pretty bad but I really think you ought to do it. If you will the lady chairman would like to fix the date. I have told her that I don't know yet just when you're coming. Could you get here a day or so before time to leave for Louisiana. Let me know as soon as you can as I promised Mrs. Hudson I'd let her know about the date.

I had thought of an autographing party at the Three Muske-teers Book shop but the woman there is such an absolute fool that I am advised against it. My advisers say that an appearance at the woman's club is far better publicity. I will arrange, I think, to have books there for the autographing.

1. This letter is missing.
2. See *CG 26*.
3. "B from Bull's Foot" appeared in the August 1936 issue of *Scribner's*; Gordon's collaborator was Nash Buckingham, a local sports expert.
4. Ford gave a lecture to a woman's club in Memphis.

CG 29. TLS. 1 l. [May? 1935] Memphis.

Dear Ford:

I write for Allen in order to get this off as soon as possible. You can find more statements of the Agrarians' position in the files of The American Review than anywhere else. Allen says read John Ransom's Happy Farmer article in an American Review of about a year ago.[1] If I were you I'd telephone Mr. Lowes[2] at the American Review office and have him send you around a file of the maga-zine. I imagine you'd get everything you want from that.

It's bad news to know there's little chance of your coming south again. We'd been hoping you all would make it in June. Leonie [Adams] told me she and her husband would come but they haven't set any date and I suppose it would be hard to get them to come at the time that suited you.

We are marking time here—at least I am; Allen is working like the Dickens—till we can leave for Benfolly which ought to be about the fifth of June. I'll certainly be glad to shake the dust of Memphis from my feet.

I hope Red finally came across with the money. I wrote him in as emphatic a way as I could several times. A note from him the other day didn't mention it. I'm hoping that meant he'd already sent it.

I have been reading Life on the Mississippi.[3] The first half of it is magnificent—I haven't been so excited over a book for years, then suddenly the whole book goes flop, just after the war. The last half might have been written by Mrs. Myrick.[4] I can't understand what happened to the man. Sold out to the Yankees, I reckon.

This is a very dull letter. I am feeling very low—haven't been able to start my novel [*None Shall Look Back*] and don't feel that I ever will. I've been trying to get started ever since I got back from Baton Rouge but no words come.

We are all well, however and trust you are both the same. Don't work too hard. Much, much love to you both. I still hope we'll see you this summer. Can't you persuade somebody else to drive you down. Isn't there some earnest Communist who'd like to investigate crime in Montgomery county? They've been coming through Memphis all year. The last one was James Rorty[5] on his way back from the Southern Writers' conference. He spent a week investigating and we had many a rousing argument by the fireside. Nathan Asch has never been heard of since he went out to live with the share croppers. I think maybe some planter or riding boss ate him.

After June 4 address us just Clarksville. Allen sends his love,

C.

1. "Happy Farmers," *American Review* 1 (5) (Oct. 1933): 513–35.
2. Marvin McCord Lowes reviewed Ford's *Provence* in the September 1935 issue of the *American Review*.
3. The first part of Mark Twain's autobiographical narrative deals with his life as a boy on the river, the second part with his return as an adult.
4. A Memphis woman whom Gordon was tutoring in the technique of novel writing.
5. A leftist journalist who had come down to investigate the conditions of sharecroppers; his visit involved the Tates, against their will and persuasion, in a political controversy (see Waldron 149–51).

CG 30. TLS. 2 ll. [Dec. 1935 and early Jan. 1936] Memphis.

Dearest Ford and Janice:

I just came across this review of "Provence" which I've had on hand for months, meaning to send—you've probably seen it long ago. I don't know where the time goes. Every now and then one of your Memphis admirers asks me when I've heard from "Mister Ford" and I am startled to reflect that I haven't heard or written. (My pupil, Mrs. Myrick, by the way, has some of your remarks from the Southern Review article[1] pinned up over her desk; she evidently thinks they will do her some sort of good, by absorption from the printer's ink doubtless.)

We've been in Memphis since September. In fact we left Benfolly shortly after you all did, case of rats leaving a sinking ship, only it was the rats not the ship who seemed to be sinking. Finding that we had to close the house we went down and lived on the Lytles[2] for the rest of the summer. It wasn't quite as bad as it sounds. They raise everything to eat on the plantation. I saw the grocery bill for seven of us (including the feed for three hundred turkeys) and it was fifteen dollars a month, so we didn't feel we were much financial burden. We had a lovely time. Andrew's father is a man who [has] great regard for the Muse and everything was run so we could get our work done—Andrew was writing a book too. We wrote all day, then at five o'clock swam in Smith's Lake for an hour then came home and had one cocktail, a wonderful supper, played a few selections on the Victrola (mostly Caruso: Nancy complained that she'd like a little Bing Crosby for a change), then fell into bed and slept eight hours, got up in the morning and went through the same routine. It was a lovely, charmed time—we all had the feeling that it was one of those things that would never come again. And alas, the Lytles are losing the plantation. In fact the sheriff served papers giving them six hours to get out while we were there. Mr. Lytle, having so high a regard for the Muse, didn't even mention the matter to us. He told the sheriff he couldn't get the volumes of the official records of the civil war off the place in six hours, much less his teams, tools etc. and they would just have to let things go on a little longer, which they did. It is a very melodramatic affair—a wicked brother in law who is determined to ruin Mr. Lytle and has managed to get his clutches on the plantation through Mr. Lytle's generosity.

We spent two weeks at Benfolly towards the end of the summer then came on here where things go on much as usual. Allen finds the school routine much less trying this year than the last and has managed to get some writing done. His poems, dedicated to you,[3] will be out in February, I think it is. The Alcestis Press, very de luxeish edition. I have been working like hell on my novel [*None Shall Look Back*] till a few days ago when I suddenly went so stale that I had to quit and took up raking the leaves off the back yard for a change. Scribner's have been putting a lot of pressure on me, promising to make it the leader on their list if I will finish it in time for spring publication. I tried very hard to do it for awhile but decided the other day I was running a chance of ruining the book, so it will just have to take its chances in the fall.

We are going to Benfolly for two weeks Christmas. Andrew and his sister are coming down and I suppose some other guests.

1936

I started this letter before Christmas but was interrupted before I could finish. And Christmas, thank God, is now over, and after a hectic ten days at Benfolly and other places we are back in the bungalow.

There's no news. I'm trying to get back to my novel—it won't be on Scribner's spring list, after all. Allen is correcting proof on his essays[4] and Nancy is trying to get down to earth after holiday excitements. Vili, the dog, who had to spend two nights in the Waller basements,[5] says he is glad to get home. I wish, Janice, you could see this dog. I believe you would leap to your pencil to perpetuate his beautiful elliptical lines. He is sweet, too, and a little calmer than he used to be.

Oh yes, there's one piece of news. Allen has written a play. Yep. The name of it is "The Turn of the Screw." He has an interpretation of that masterpiece,[6] which applied, works out amazingly in a play. The idea— you may divine it—is that there never were any apparitions, they were all manifestations of let us say the governess' baser self. The children instead of being corrupted by the wicked valet and governess did nothing but learn a few bad words from them but learned instead evil from the really high minded governess who was trying to "save" them. Whether true or false it is interesting to examine the story in the light of this opinion. Every single sentence almost is capable of a double meaning. And all this before anybody had heard of Freud! It's the most terrible thing, I believe, I've ever read. I don't know, really, whether an audience could stand it in play form. Anyhow, it's done—of course it will have to be "doctored" and we're going to see if anything can be done with it.

I haven't even dared to speculate on whether you all will come over but do for heaven's sake let us know if there's any chance. We think of you so often and want so much to see you. I've got so I can't write letters—this novel is a devil. God knows whether I can ever finish it. It's such a nightmare that my mind never gets free from it—so letters from me would be no kindness. I wonder, though, whether you are in Paris or Toulon, how things are going. Do, if you can get around to it, write and let us have some news.

Allen—and Nancy—send their love to you both. A happy, happy New Year,

as ever,
Caroline

1531 Forrest Avenue

The dog is a dachshund, and very difficult. Dr. Sanborn[7] told us he was strictly a one man dog but it's turned out one woman. He can't bear anybody but me and growls whenever Allen comes in the room. He's slowly getting a little more manageable, though.

1. "Techniques," published in the July 1935 issue of the *Southern Review*.
2. Andrew Lytle's father owned a plantation, Cornsilk, in Guntersville, Alabama.
3. *The Mediterranean and Other Poems* (1936); with the dedication "To Ford Madox Ford who gave me the poem."
4. *Reactionary Essays on Poetry and Ideas* (1936).
5. James Waller, a friend of the Tates, lived in Nashville; he was a contributor to the symposium *Who Owns America*.
6. Henry James's story of 1898.
7. Herbert Sanborn, chairman of the philosophy department at Vanderbilt, was a great lover of dogs.

~

1936–1937

CG 31. **TL. 3 ll. [Sept. 1936] Monteagle.**

Dearest Ford:

Every day this summer, last winter, too, for that matter I have been going to write to you and Janice but I have been working all the moments I wasn't in a state of collapse getting ready to work again for two years now. Before I say anything else let me give you a message—the message I was going to send the next morning after we wrote that post card in Olivet, Michigan.

Dorothea Brande says next time you have a book come out for God's sake have the publishers send her the proofs. She is an ardent admirer of your works and says she is very much distressed by the lousy proof reading they've had. She's expert at reading proof, having run the American Mercury for some years and helped run the American Review of later years. Perhaps I'd better tell you who she is in case you ever have any communications from her. She's first of all, a very erudite and charming lady, weighing, I should say two hundred pounds. She's been desperately poor for years and last year she put her tongue in her plump cheek and wrote a formula for success book called "Wake up and Live." It was selling four thousand copies a week all last summer—God knows what its total is by this time. She also wrote a mystery story called "Most Beautiful Lady," a darned good job. She's marrying Seward Collins who edits the American Review this month—so now you know all I can tell you about her. We met her at the middle western writers' conference in Michigan this summer, and liked her tremendously.

It was so good to hear from you two, though you sound a little tired in your letter. The trouble about letters is that you can't write to your friends when you're working and when you're not working you're too depressed to write. I have thought of you often, every day, in fact, but I've been desperately pressed getting this novel [*None Shall Look Back*] ready. As it is, I'm too late by a season. Margaret Mitchell's "Gone with the Wind" a civil war novel of one thousand pages, came out this spring and gobbled up all the trade. Anthony Adverse[1] as a seller looks sick beside it. I don't believe any book ever sold like it before—the formula is sound, a Civil war Becky Sharp,[2] and Lord how they're gobbling it up! I finished my book, or thought I'd finished it, in July and we then set off for Michigan and later New York—Allen had some lectures to deliver at Columbia or we'd never have got there, of course. We were in Michigan two weeks—it seemed years, those kindly middle westerners just drain you—then we were in New York two weeks, I believe. We stayed most of the time in Mark Van Doren's apartment which he had kindly turned over to us, on Bleecker street. There weren't very many people in town we knew. Still it was pretty exhausting just getting around to see a few people. I hadn't been in New York for years, except a very brief stay on that Guggenheim excursion. I found it much nicer, that is to say more like Paris, than it was when we lived there. Side walks restaurants and cafes have made the change, of course and I believe there are more trees, certainly more gardens, so called, to eat in. Everybody we knew was doing practically the same thing they were doing the last time we saw them. That is the extraordinary thing to me about New York. Everybody seems to remain static. Nathan Asch, strapped and living in the country, was making plans, trying to get his wife and child to town—just what he was doing six years ago, different wife, of course, and I believe there was no child at the time. Malcolm [Cowley] was building a house in the country. We went out to Tory Valley where we used to live and found Bill [Brown] and Sue [Jenkins Brown] sitting in the same attitudes we left them in many years ago. I believe they have been separated and reunited half a dozen times since we saw them but there they were looking as if not a moment had rolled over their heads. We spent a week with the Mark [and Dorothy] Van Dorens at their place in Connecticut. We are very fond of both of them and had a lovely time there but that whole country makes me a little nervous, combined pleasure park and graveyard—we were glad to get south of Princeton where the country begins to get that ragged, cultivated look again. Carl Van Doren[3] came over once while we were there. He is writing his memoirs. I believe Irita[4] was married that week, I forget the man's name.

Perkins, at Scribner's, says the depression is over—but he is worrying now over the European war he thinks will certainly come. He thought my book needed a little more rounding out. All the minor characters aren't accounted for and he complained I killed off too many young men. I came home, killed off one and a half more young men and hope to have the manuscript ready to send off next week. I am pretty well soaked in gore by this time, having treated of the siege of Fort Donelson, the battle of Chickamauga, the battle of Okolona, the battle of Brice's Cross Roads as well as a few cavalry skirmishes. I think my thesis is sound but I don't think you'll like the book much. It's been too hastily done—so much of my energy had to go into mastering manoeuvres—and the writing on the whole is poor. There is one chapter, though, that I believe is good—the women on the battle field, and another short passage, the prelude to the battle of Chickamauga. I had to use every device I ever heard of or could invent—the material I had was so complicated and so resistant to handling. Some very pretty problems came up. How often I wished for you! One was the problem of getting enough variety into the battle scenes. I hope I succeeded. I made each battle do something that advanced the plot, all except Chickamauga which I portrayed as my grand spectacle in six sections. Well, enough of that. It will be bad enough when you have to read it. I doubt whether you'll be able to.

We stopped at Benfolly this year only long enough to say hello to the cow and the Normans and came on to Monteagle. Andrew's family have a large—a baronial—log cabin here and we have settled down to stay till cold weather runs us out. We like it very much. This is an old fashioned summer resort, but most of the people are gone and we have the mountain to ourselves. It is on the top of a mountain but we have no view unless we walk to "the point" for it. Mr. [Robert] Lytle has sent up a cook from the plantation and he comes up every Saturday with his car loaded with chickens, vegetables, eggs and butter. Polly, Andrew's sister, does the housekeeping. I have no excuse not to work but I am awfully tired of working. Nancy is going to school in Chattanooga, at her great aunt Margaret's. They begged to have her and it is much better for her to be there. Allen would have had to drive twenty five miles a day getting her back and forth.

We are planning to go to Mexico in January, lured by the persistent report that a dollar is worth three dollars and sixty cents there. I doubt if we make it, though, unless my book sells. Scribner's made great promises when they were hoping I'd get it ready last spring but I fear they're rather dashed now by "Gone with the Wind." The hell of it is that Bobbs-Merrill tell me they *know* they could sell it.

I am collecting some kodak pictures to send you. I find, already printed, one of the cabin. The gallery runs on all four sides of the house. If you are in working mood you set up your typewriter table in a spot that's not much frequented and go to it. My "study" I've marked with an arrow, just around the corner of the house. Of course when cold weather comes we'll have to desert the veranda and huddle up in the rooms. There are four abovestairs, one in each corner of the halls which go through in the shape of a cross, so that in the summer time we have four living rooms at our disposal.

Allen was very much pleased by your letter[5]—but he will be writing you himself. His lectures went over very well at Columbia—he says he had two very respectable looking old colored women in gold rimmed specs in his audience.

Allen is sending the Mercury poem[6] to Warren at the Southern Review. They have a perfect deluge of poetry on hand just now, having just concluded a contest—but if the book[7] is published in England I shouldn't think the date of publication here would matter. I will let Allen tell you what he thinks of the poem—he being better fitted to do it than I.

Janice is very kind to lump the Tates as both friend and family.[8] I wish you two were here with us now. It is dreadful, always having seas divide us. Bill Brown swore that he, or perhaps it was somebody else, saw you on the street in New York this spring but we knew you wouldn't come to New York without letting us know—though Katherine Anne, the worm, actually did! The only person I can hear of who saw her on her recent trip was Genevieve Taggard.[9] I can understand, though, how, having gone all the way to Texas and back she wouldn't feel like seeing anybody in the world.

The last part of this letter is doubtless a little confused—I started drinking whiskey and soda on the third page. I am just so tired from that book it takes two drinks to get me up to anything like normal.

Much love to you both. Don't let us wait so long to hear from each other again,

Always,

Monteagle, Tennessee

Just found some more pictures. The one of Nancy and me isn't so good—the sun was in our eyes—but isn't it splendid of the Count of Isarthal? That is just the way he looks, highly intelligent. The other day I went to Nashville. He wouldn't touch his food until I came back at eleven o'clock at night. He does not really care for anybody in the world except me—Allen says I am weak minded to be so easily flattered but it [is] rare to meet such devotion in this life.

1. Best-seller romance about the Napoleonic era (1933) by the American novelist Hervey Allen.
2. The ruthless and scheming heroine of William Makepeace Thackeray's *Vanity Fair* (1847–48).
3. Professor at Columbia University, editor and critic.
4. Irita Van Doren, editor of the *New York Herald Tribune Books*; earlier married to Carl Van Doren.
5. Ford's letter to Allen Tate of September 6, 1936 (*Letters* 255–59), in which he praised Tate's book of poems.
6. Ford's "Latin Quarter," published in the September 1936 issue of the *London Mercury*.
7. Ford's *Collected Poems*, published in October 1936.
8. In Ford's letter of September 6, 1936, he quoted Biala's comment on the Tates; see *Letters* 257.
9. Poet and close friend of Katherine Anne Porter since the 1920s.

CG 32. TLS. 1 l. [Nov. 1936] Monteagle.

Dearest Ford:

SUCH NEWS![1] We can hardly wait to see you. But before I say anything else there is a business matter I should have mentioned to you before this.

Last summer as I may have told you we attended a writers' conference at Olivet, Michigan. The conference was a great success and is now an annual affair. Joe Brewer, erstwhile publisher, is president of the college and is doing some rather remarkable things with it. His brightest idea so far is to create a chair of letters or whatever you'd call it and get you to fill it. He asked us last summer whether we thought that you would fall in with the idea. We told him we couldn't say but we thought that you might not be averse to spending a year in America. It would of course be very fitting to have you start the thing off in view of your editorship of transatlantic[2] and everything else you've done for middle western letters. I should, really, have written you before this but until the other day Joe didn't know where he'd get the money and I hated to approach you when we had nothing tangible to offer. Now Joe writes that he has got or can certainly get together $1500 for the year. It's not much but then there's no work attached to the job. Do write me that you'd look on the proposition favorably. Joe will be in New York around the thirteenth of December and will doubtless see you then. I want, however, to be able to write him that you look favorably on the idea before he goes ahead with getting the money.

Olivet is a very pleasant little elm shaded village. The college people are pleasant. Joe himself really is a fine fellow. His idea, I think, is to have next year's conference July 9—to July 24 and the ideal thing, of course, would be to have you there to start things off. I am so hoping you'll fall in with the plan. We hope in case

you do accept that you'll come down and stay with us till time to
go to Olivet. Andrew also sends an invitation. We have many houses
on our hands at present, Benfolly, of course, and the log cabin at
Monteagle which is even more convenient than Benfolly. The Lytles
have also just got back from the wicked brother-in-law their plantation.[3] The government is flooding that valley but the houses on
the plantation will be left, on a forty mile long lake. Mr. Lytle
wants to establish a sort of colony, build cabins and he will supply
us with vegetables etc. which he raises in five and six acre lots anyhow—we could just nibble off a half acre of onions to pleasure
him. Do try to stay in America a year, anyhow. And please, let me
know as soon as you can what you think of the idea so I can wire
Joe. He expected me to have consulted you before this about it.

By the way Dorothea Brande, author of Wake up and Live and
some better books (a mystery novel, "Most Beautiful Lady") has
been very active in getting the money together. She is one of your
most ardent admirers. Again by the way she is married to Seward
Collins, editor of The American Review.

An incoherent letter, I fear, but I am writing between breaths. Have
been working on my novel [*None Shall Look Back*], adding more chapters to round the thing out and still have one more to do.

Much love from all of us to you both,

as ever,

caroline

MONTEAGLE, TENNESSEE

Do be nice to Joe Brewer. He has the greatest admiration for you.
Of course he wants to put this through as a way of increasing the
college's prestige. At the same time he has a genuine feeling that your
great services to American letters ought to have some tangible recognition and he has tried very hard to do his bit towards that.

You understand there are no set classes. You merely lend your
presence for a year. Of course you'd have to advise aspiring writers
but you do such a hell of a lot of that anyhow.

Please communicate with me immediately by letter so that I
can pass whatever word it is on to Joe.

[Autograph note,[4] presumably telegram from FMF, drafted by him.
First draft:] Caroline Tate Monteagle Quite inclined consider
favourably but cannot commit myself without knowing further details. Pleased to see Brewer [Second draft:] Mrs. Allen Tate Monteagle
Tenn Quite inclined consider favourably but cannot decide naturally
without further details. Janice fears climate What is distance between
Olivet Monteagle. In any case hope to see you soon Much love

1. Evidently refers to a letter or other message that is missing.
2. The *transatlantic review* (1924), edited by Ford in Paris.
3. By a court decision of August 1936 Robert Lytle got the Cornsilk plantation back from his half-sister Andrewena Robertson and her husband.
4. At the end of this letter Ford drafted a telegram to Gordon; see *FMF 13*, which prints the fuller version of two drafts.

FMF 13. Draft of telegram. [End of Nov. or early Dec.? 1936] [New York]

Mrs. Allen Tate Monteagle Tenn Quite inclined consider favourably but cannot decide naturally without further details. Janice fears climate What is distance between Olivet Monteagle. In any case hope to see you soon Much love[1]

1. Draft of telegram jotted down on *CG 32*.

CG 33. TL. 2 ll. [Dec. 1936] Monteagle.

Dear Ford and Janice:

I was glad to have your telegram.[1] I also had an ecstatic telegram from Joe Brewer who was on his way to New York. He was delighted to know you all were there. Doubtless you have seen him by this time. We don't at all urge this thing on you, you know. But when Joe suggested it we thought that at least it might finance or partly finance a period of vegetation.

It is five hundred and fifty miles from Olivet to Benfolly—too far alas for week ending. We hope, however, that you all will get down to see us in the spring. The Lytles have just left—they have got back their plantation after much lawing and are moving there—and Allen and I have the log cabin at Monteagle to ourselves. They may rent it in the summer but it is ours until June. We plan to stay on here till late spring, anyhow. It is too much of a job to open Benfolly in the winter and living somehow costs twice as much there as it does here. We hope you'll come down. There is plenty of room. It is a log cabin but the bedrooms are ceiled or whatever you call it and are very warm. The halls are unheated except for the end of one which we have curtained off and ceiled with handsome Cimabuean blue builders' paper to make a living room. It has a splendid fire place and is comfortable except in the most severe weather, and tolerable then. The village is ten minutes' walk away. Bus station, western union etc. We have electricity and running water and for heat handsome log fires. We are crazy about living here and I think you all might like it too. We'll have at least one cold spell in January or February but you never have that dreary drizzling that you get in Paris.

Allen and I are leaving here tomorrow to go by Chattanooga and pick up Nancy who's at school there, then on to Merry Mont for a few days, back to Chattanooga and thence to Richmond where Allen is delivering a paper to some sort of academic gathering. We'll be back here around the first of the year, however and hope to settle down.

My book is coming out in late January.[2] Had to change the title at the last minute because Metro Goldwyn owns "The Cup of Fury." We finally decided on "None Shall Look Back" which was the best we could do. Nahum or some prophet. "Stand, stand shall they cry yet none shall look back."[3] Scribner's are really pushing this book. I have faint hopes of making some money. Have an agent working on the movie sale. She said several companies approached her about it a month or two ago. I can't really think it would go in the movies, though. The same agent, by the way, asked if I'd take a short term writing contract on the coast if she could get it for me. I said yes, of course, needing the money, but she hasn't landed anything as yet. That would be the only thing that would take us away from Monteagle this spring and that seems unlikely to come off. However even if we left you could be just as comfortable here as the village is so near you don't really need a car.

I forgot to say that the cabin is quite comfortably furnished, with beds enough for a regiment and everything else one needs for house keeping, including electric heater in the bathroom, electric grills etc.

Do write when you get a chance and tell us what your plans are, how long you expect to stay in New York and so on. Any time you could come down here would suit us. We will be here from January first on.

Allen sends his best. Love to you both,

as ever,

MONTEAGLE, TENNESSEE

Mail will be forwarded from here while we're gone.

1. See *CG 32* and *FMF 13*.
2. *None Shall Look Back* was published in February 1937.
3. "But Nineveh is of old like a pool of water: yet they shall flee away. Stand, stand, shall they cry; but none shall look back" (Nahum 2:8).

FMF 14. TLS. 2 ll. Jan. 15, 1937. New York.

January 15, 1937

Dearest Caroline,

I am not going to say that I haven't written you for a long time because both our correspondences are always in that condition. We ought to agree to a code word with that meaning. We've been here as you know, going on to two months now. We purpose stopping here until April. We are not quite certain whether that means the beginning or the end of the month. Then, if you permit it, we purpose to come down and stop with you for a little while and then to move about in the South until July when I promised [Joseph] Brewer that I would go to his conference at Olivet and if youall are coming along that will make it so much the better. After Olivet we purpose to go back to Toulon and to buy a little property with a small shack on it and gradually dig ourselves in and settle down to work for a year or so. At any rate I have taken on enough to keep me going until well into 1940.

With regard to Brewer I really don't know. The more I think of it, the more cold feet I get—principally about the weather and also a good deal over the social conditions. I rather fancy that to be shut up in a small community under the microscopic scrutiny of small town people would be pretty insupportable. However, I told Brewer that we could not say anything definite until after July when we've been to the conference. In a larger place the conditions might be almost ideal. We'll talk about it when we see you.

Janice has been working fairly well since we've been here. She's to have an exhibition on the 23rd of February. Why don't you come up to see it? We could give you and Allen a shake-down if you did.

You know, my dear, your letter is rather inscrutable. You sent us the map of a cottage without explaining why. Has perhaps a former letter in which you invited us to occupy it gone astray? It looks as if that must be the case from other phrases in the letter.

Your cousin [Cath] Wilds is a charming person. We have done our best to make her and that imitation Yorkshireman, Mr. [Harold] Cash, who must really be from the North Riding, where Tietjens grow,[1] as welcome as we could. She's trying to get a job and we have introduced her to several people who might be useful. But the tendency of everyone, somehow, is to say that they will be charmed to have her but they are full and then they recommend her to someone else. She has given us most of your news, but it seems to be so scattered and diverse and compounded of suddenly undertaken expeditions that it seems very difficult to picture exactly where you are or what you are doing. There seems to be a magazine and dark mysteries. At any rate Miss Wilds starts out hinting darkly at a magazine and intrigues and then checks herself suddenly and says, "Perhaps I oughtn't to say that."

My book of THE GREAT TRADE ROUTE ought to be out by the middle of February, but the Oxford Press never cease remember-

ing that it was founded in 1460 so that their idea of doing anything on the expected date seems to [be] abhorrent to them. I have
also finished and corrected the proofs for my next book [*Portraits
from Life*] which consists of the things that were running in The
Mercury, for Houghton Mifflin and I am just going to start on
another enormous work [*The March of Literature*].

Janice said to send her love and also that she was prepared to
send you a small cat if you wanted one. The janitor's cat here has
just had five kittens which she wishes to reserve from drowning.

Guests bursting in

All sorts of love

F. M. F.

1. Christopher Tietjens is the main protagonist of Ford's tetralogy *Parade's
End* (1924–26, 1928; published in one volume in 1950).

CG 34. TLS. 2 ll. [Jan.? 1937] Monteagle.

My dearest Ford:

The trouble with you is that you do not read my letters. However, it is of no moment as there was nothing of importance in that
letter except that along with the map I sent you and Janice an explicit invitation to come and occupy the Lytle cottage on top of
Cumberland mountain whenever you got ready. We had hoped
you'd be here before April. However we will still be here then and
the mountain is heavenly in April—if Janice doesn't do something
swell with the mountain laurel I shall be disappointed.

It is good news about the exhibition.[1] I wish we could be there to
see it but we will not be moving from here until some sort of ship
comes in. We were in Washington New Year's and would have come
on to see you all then if our money hadn't run out. As it was we barely
made it home.

I am so glad you will be with us at Olivet, I should think we could
all drive over together. It is really very pleasant, driving through the
middle west then—it's positively golden with grain and the lakes are
lovely. However we shall count on seeing you long before then. If you
have any work to do you really should come on down to Monteagle. It
is the best place to work I know. The roof does leak but only in the
halls and one only wanders through the halls. The rooms where one
lives and works are tight and can be made very warm—you will probably pant for breath in them. We can even offer Society. The University of the South is only six miles away. There is plenty of Society
there, with a strong episcopal flavour. The dominant dowagers all have

bishops or Confederate generals for fathers; sometimes they have a father that is both and then there is something doing. We have stayed out of this social spate, knowing it was too swift for us and have permitted ourselves only one University friend,[2] an agreeable rattle who comes once or twice a week and tells us tales that would curl our hair if we hadn't already read it in Trollope[3] or Cranford.[4] But as I say we stay pretty much out of all that.

Allen is writing a novel [*The Fathers*]! He fought hard against it but had to come to it at last. He is deep in it and now that he's taken the plunge is really enjoying himself. Andrew, resting between novels, has taken up cabinet making and is contemplating a trip to Hollywood as soon as he gets his cedar chest finished. I am writing—at least I think I am writing a detective story. My detective is an old fashioned Southern lawyer, an Agrarian Sherlock Holmes who solves crimes by knowing everything about his region—he knows the pedigree of every white person, colored person, horse, dog and mule in his community. He has a colored Watson named Beauchamp—I think a colored Watson could be very handy, for negroes, as Sherwood Anderson showed us in "Dark Laughter" always know everything worth knowing in any community. The real point, though, is the detective's approach. These modern detectives—Philo Vance and so on—know a little about everything and none of it related to anything. I'll probably never finish it but it's fun triggering with the thing after two years of the civil war.

I'm glad you all are seeing something of Cath [Wilds] and Harold [Cash]. Cath is a charming child. She has some talent too, though she may not ever do anything, won't work. Harold is a fine fellow. By the way we've always said he reminded us of you. Yes, I quite see the Yorkshireman in him.

Must get to work. Tell Janice to work the cat off on somebody else. I had eight at Benfolly last count, probably sixteen by this time.

The magazine of which Cath darkly speaks was a magazine to be called "New America," dedicated to Agrarianism. The patron was secured, roped and tied by Herbert Agar and then suddenly the magazine turned into what Allen calls "a liberal-eclectic hash." The Agrarians withdrew, saddened but not surprised. When big money comes on the scene Agrarianism usually flies out of the window.

Much love to you both and looking forward to seeing you

Caroline

MONTEAGLE, TENNESSEE

1. Biala's show at the Passedoit Gallery in New York, February 23, 1937.

2. Probably Samuel Monk, a member of the English department.

3. Anthony Trollope (1815–1882), prolific English writer, best known for a series of novels set in his fictional Barsetshire.

4. A novel (1853) by Elizabeth Cleghorn Gaskell (1810–1865), depicting life in an English village.

CG 35. TLS. 1 l. [Feb. 1937] Chattanooga.

Dearest Ford:

The book[1] has come and we are reading it between us, in snatches. That is, the one who has just snatched reads. Allen, who is pampering himself horribly these days on the grounds that he is writing a novel [*The Fathers*], has had it most of the time. He reports that the opening, particularly, arouses his admiration. He says it is masterly. He is going to write something about it for the Southern Review, or rather I believe he has it in mind to do an article, called, say Ford Madox Ford: A Portrait and discuss your work in general. But to return to the present book, it is a beautiful book, full of the usual miraculous cadences. I like the part about the Indians, some nice points are brought out there, and all the Walter Atterbury part is swell.[2] (I must set you right on gar-fish or grinnell: you cannot make soup out of them. It would be like stirring up a cocktail out of fire and brimstone.) As for the drawings, they are swell. The jacket is the best Janice has done, I think. I do not *like* these drawings as well, on the whole, as the Provence ones but that is because of the subject. Provence just naturally gets more out of Janice. I keep it around all the time where I can look at it.

Perkins has sent me a copy of your review[3] of "None Shall Look Back." I am overwhelmed by it and suspect uneasily that that imagination of yours has run away with you. I fear the book lacks that Olympian ease you ascribe to it, in fact I think it is a pretty sweaty book . . . but I am proud to have evoked such beautiful sentences from you. Thanks a thousand times.

We are spending two weeks in Chattanooga to look after the children—one of them is Nancy—while my aunt and uncle[4] vacation in Florida. Allen pounds away at his novel and I am trying to get myself geared up to finish "A Morning's Favour." We will be back on the mountain[5] in a few more days and glad to be there.

Love from both of us and thanks to you both for the beautiful book, and for the review which has sentences in it as beautiful as those of the book,

as ever,

caroline

Perkins was tremendously pleased with your review as why shouldn't he be!

The enclosed review was written by a young squirt from Arkansas who is just back from Oxford.—A.T.

1. *Great Trade Route* was published on January 12, 1937.
2. Ford describes how as a child he and his nurse's grandson Walter Atterbury "made the most astounding voyages on the Spanish Main— in the kitchen table turned upside down" (*Great Trade Route* [New York: Oxford Univ. Press, 1937], 9). He writes about Indians and their culture in a chapter called "Hoes," and on garfish—"only fit for making soup"— in a section entitled "Below the Line," that is, the Mason-Dixon Line (*Great Trade Route* 349).
3. For Ford's review, see the introduction, xxvii.
4. While going to school in Chattanooga Nancy was staying with Margaret (Pidie) Meriwether and Paul Campbell.
5. That is, at the Lytles' log cabin in Monteagle.

CG 36. TLS. 2 ll. [End of Feb.? 1937] Monteagle.

My dearest Ford:

Fine to have your letter.[1] The amusing thing about your book [*Great Trade Route*]—in the South—is that Allen is given the credit of converting you to Agrarianism. You are supposed to have sat at his feet— one reviewer describes the moment of your conversion, on the upper gallery at Benfolly. I suppose this sort of thing is no more absurd than the average review but it is a pretty good joke on you who must have been a practising Agrarian when Allen was in his cradle. I've noticed, however, that the book is having splendid reviews, which is pleasant. NSB,[2] on the contrary, seems to be getting panned good and hard. Well, I was due to get it in the neck this time.

Our movements are more certain than usual. We will stay at the Lytle cabin until time to go to Olivet. If the Lytles should have a chance to rent the cabin we'd move out, of course, to Benfolly. But there is little chance of their renting it. Andrew's grandmother, aunts and great aunts usually come up for the month of July but we would be ready to go to Olivet then so that works out all right. As I have told you repeatedly there is plenty of room and the accomodations are adequate though not luxurious. We count on your coming. It is a good place to work and in May a pleasant place to be. The mountain is lovely then.

As for the artists' colony it exists as yet only in Mr. [Robert] Lytle's dreams. The Lytles have been financially involved for years and have just recovered possession of their plantation.[3] They intended to start enlarging the log house there in February but found that the road around the lake would go through the house. (The government is taking all but two hundred and fifty acres for a lake.) They have to wait until the government engineers say what they are going to do before they start building. But Mr. Lytle hopes that some of us will come there to stay. He is in the lumber business and can put up cabins very cheaply, using his own timber. I don't know whether the colony could be going by next fall but certainly it ought to be started within the year. We have never talked things over in detail. I rather think Mr. Lytle intends putting up some guest houses himself. But any of us who wanted a modicum of independence could build our own cabin on that land and it would give Mr. Lytle great pleasure to furnish us with the overflowings from his truck gardens. He raises tomatoes, onions etc. by the acres. I am distrustful of all colonies, or even associations of intimate friends but in this case I think such a plan would work. This is because of the peculiar nature of the Lytles—they are the most hospitable and amiable of people. We, of course, hate to leave Benfolly but if the Lytle concern gets going we'd probably be drawn in. By the way if you could bring yourself to stay in America you could have our cabin at Benfolly. It is charmingly situated now in the locust grove—we moved it there for Manson [Radford]. There are only two rooms but we have always intended to add a large room on in the back which would make it very pleasant. We could add on such a room very cheaply and would be so glad to turn the cabin over to you. Allen says I have cabinitis. I am always seeing how nicely one could live in a cabin. The Benfolly house is one of the damnedest houses I ever saw, all that space and none of it in the right place. An even more practical suggestion would be to add dormer windows to make the third floor habitable—it is at present a black hole of Calcutta as you must know from sad experience. But if you had air there those two upper rooms would be nice. Anyhow if you all decide to stay in America houses and even lands will be provided.

By the way Vanderbilt is having some sort of regional writers' conference (academic affair) April 28. Do try to get here in time for that. I'm afraid there's no expense money, at least John Ransom—who doesn't know as yet that you're coming this way—said he had none to give out when he wrote the other day. Allen says please start growing an imperial. He is building you up as a Southern colonel and wants his disciple to do him credit.

Allen has one third of his novel [*The Fathers*] finished and proceeds steadily. "When Bull onct takes holt heaven and yarth can't make him let go." ("Hoosier Schoolmaster."[4] Bet you don't know who wrote it.)

Love to you both and Manson and Rose [Radford] when you see them, also Cath [Wilds] and the imitation Yorkshireman [Harold Cash]. Quite a little circle of Southern colonels you have there. Tell

Cath that her family is delighted to know that she has a job in the religious department of Harpers and so am I,

as ever,

caroline

1. This letter is missing.
2. *None Shall Look Back.*
3. See *CG 32.*
4. *The Hoosier Schoolmaster* (1871), novel by Edward Eggleston (1837–1902).

CG 37. TLS. 1 l. [Late Mar.? 1937] Monteagle.

Dearest Ford:

I have just finished PORTRAITS FROM LIFE. I read it very slowly, savoring every word. If anybody else had written it I'd have a lot to say about the style—and beautiful tone—of the book but in your case such remarks are almost an impertinence, one has come so to take it for granted that you will write beautifully. I can only say that I think it is one of your better books and written better than I'd expected it to be. (You should pause here and reflect on exactly what I mean by the phrase "better than I'd expected.") I think, too, that you have got something into it that one can never *expect* in a book, even a book by you. You have told many of these stories before and it is not that the versions you give here are better than former versions—yes, they really are done more tellingly—but you have got a passion into the telling. I don't suppose you'll ever treat of these particular subjects again and that realization has given an edge to the whole book. It's as if you felt you were saying the last word—the very last word you could have to say—about these men, and were saying it for posterity, as I think you have.

We have had to change our plans a little. The Nelson ladies[1] are coming to the cottage for June so we have decided to go on to Benfolly April 25. So we'll receive you there instead of here. It would have been nice to have the month here on the mountain but that would involve moving twice for you all and I don't think it's worth it.

Love to you both. We look forward to seeing you the first of May. If for any reason you change your plans let me know. I want to be sure to get to Benfolly in time to have things straight before you come,

as ever,

Caroline

Monteagle

NSB has sold over five thousand to date which is pretty good for me.

1. See *CG 36*.

CG 38. CG to JB. TLS. 2 ll. [Apr.? 1937] [Monteagle]

Dear Janice:

Your letter[1] has just come. By this time you must have got my letter announcing what to me is sad news that we will have to receive you at Benfolly instead of Monteagle. I have, alas, another sadness to report. We had thought we would have our cabin at Benfolly available for overflow room this summer but find that we will simply have to put our tenants, the Normans in it. The cabin in the woods has become uninhabitable even for them. It is a damned nuisance but there just isn't any choice; they are absolutely dependent on us and have taken care of the place splendidly for two years.

There remains for us the Benfolly house. You know its geography, one of the damnedest houses in the world to my notion. Still in its way it's elastic. Yes, we can squeeze the sister-in-law[2] in, and we would be delighted to have her come, of course. She will have to stay in Nancy's room—it is the room you all stayed in when you were last there. I shall put you and Ford in the bedroom on the middle floor. And I can turn the parlor over to one of you to work in and the dining room to the other. I am going to work in the garage. I learned this trick from Andrew who works always en plein air. The garage will make a swell study. I would give it to you for a studio but I don't believe the light would be right. We haven't a decent north light on the place as a matter of fact. I imagine the dining room would be a better room for you than the parlor but you and Ford can decide between you. I have used both of these rooms as a study and they are really quite private. In summer we always take all our company to the upper gallery and nobody ever goes in the parlor. There is a possibility that we can also have the basement bedroom for use—if I can get a cook from one of the adjoining farms. If I can't I will have to import from Memphis the dour Rosy who will have to stay in that bedroom off the kitchen. It would be swell if we could have that extra bedroom; it too makes a grand study, very quiet and cool. I forgot to state that Allen and I will sleep on the top floor, in that room across from the one you all stayed in. If you will study this plan carefully you will see that we will all have really good working quarters and our sleeping quarters while not luxurious won't be any worse than New York apartments usually provide.

I will try to find an easel for you in Clarksville. I imagine I might be able to. At any rate I will let you know immediately after I get there. We want to get there a full week before you all arrive in order to get the house in order and scour the country for a cook. I can make no promises for the cuisine. If Rosy comes we will just have to rock along in our usual way. If she doesn't I'll probably have a green girl. You and Ford when you long for your Provencale dishes can just go in the kitchen and cook them yourselves, only you will find few of the materials in Clarksville.

Leonie Adams and her husband have talked of driving down at various times but they have a place in the country now and I imagine they won't want to leave it. I haven't thought of anybody else who'd be likely to come but I'll let you know if I do. How about Cath Wilds and her beau? Will they be thinking of coming home about that time? They both drive. Cath might know some Chattanooga student who'd be coming south though May is not the time for student migrations.

As for the library. There is a very poor library, with a few standard reference books in the normal school in Clarksville. The Vanderbilt library is forty miles away now. There is a new road straight as an arrow from Clarksville to Nashville which makes us almost suburban. We drive it in forty five minutes. It really makes a lot of difference. One can go to a party in Nashville and not have to spend the night or drive up for dinner. Ford can get anything Vanderbilt Library has, of course. The librarians there are angels.

I've mentioned all the things that come to mind about living quarters. I hope you remember the house well enough to be able to tuck us all in imagination. I don't think the loss of the cabin is going to inconvenience us seriously. I think we can all be pretty comfortable and as we will all four be working hard we'll be the less likely to get in each other's way. I am working like a fiend trying to have my book [*The Garden of Adonis*] almost finished before you all come. Scribner's insist it must be ready for fall publication. Yesterday I wrote eleven pages, the biggest day's work I've ever done in a day.

I have understood all along, of course, that you all will stay with us till time to go to Olivet. I thought we would all drive over together. We will have to take Nancy. She is beginning to be a little bitter about being parked off somewhere away from her parents. We will also have to take Vili, the dachshund but he is a charming travelling companion. We will have to travel light and parcel post most of our luggage ahead but you and Ford are famous at that. I think I can manage with one small bag for the three Tates. The sister-in-law? But she wouldn't be going to Olivet, would she?

I will re-capitulate: I can provide you with a very indifferent cuisine, fairly comfortable sleeping quarters and one large and private room apiece to work in. Allen will work in his study. So come ahead. We may not all be together again for another year. I feel sure you'll be able to work at Benfolly. I shall make it my business to see that you can. Yes, you can pay part of the grocery bill! We are not, thank God, going to be as hard up as we were last time you were there. My book [*None Shall Look Back*] has sold over 5000 copies, with good re-orders in, Perkins says. If it does as well in England we'll have enough to live on for a year which will be luxury.

Love to you both,

as ever,

caroline

Nancy will have two single beds in her room. Wally can have one of those if she doesn't mind bunking with the infant. The alternative is a cot in Allen's study but she'd still have to keep her clothes upstairs. I'm putting the three Tates on that floor so that I can keep my clothes in Nancy's big closet in the hall. There is also a bath there which we four could share. You and Ford could have the bath on the lower floor, inconvenient but you always have to traipse up or down to the bath in that house. I am fixing Nancy's room up for her according to her girlish fancy and can't turn her out—in a moment of maternal abandon I promised to let her have her own room this summer "even if Mr. Ford and Janice came." But the middle floor bedroom is really more comfortable for guests anyhow. If you find after you get here that the garage will do for a studio we can switch but the dining room if it has a decent enough light is really quite private in summer—nobody goes there except to eat. Nancy, by the way, will be pleased to have Wally for room mate. She loves to hang around grown up ladies. I'm sorry we can't offer Wally more private quarters but Nancy is a very good inoffensive child and won't be much bother.

1. This letter is missing.
2. Wally Tworkov, married to Biala's brother Jack Tworkov; she was to serve as Ford's secretary.

1938–1939

CG 39. CG to JB. TLS. 1 l. [June 1938] [Greensboro]

Dear Janice:

I have been writing to you all—in my mind's eye—for weeks, months in fact but we've been in our usual stew. Allen is within fifty pages of finishing his novel [*The Fathers*]—and as you may imagine he takes writing a novel hard. I never realized before what it is to be married to a novelist.

As it happens we know exactly where what papers Ford left at Benfolly are. There was a stack of papers in the lower compartments of the combination desk and book case in the dining room. We discussed what to do with them when we left and Allen said "Let's leave them exactly where they are and then we'll know if they need them." I'd intended to tell you about them before this but we left Benfolly in great haste. We are now leaving North Carolina in great haste, Allen having decided that he's run out of details for his next chapter and wanting to utilize the dry period on the road. We are leaving here Thursday and should be at Merry Mont Friday night. Will go over to Benfolly Saturday morning and communicate with you at once. I don't know what is in that batch of papers but I do know that the batch is intact.

We are not going to stay at Bfolly this summer—Allen has never been able to work there and it's too dangerous to try it with the novel almost done. We've rented a cottage at Cornwall, Connecticut—from the niece of Henry Ward Beecher.[1] (I hope his spirit does not haunt the mound.) There's no electricity or running water but that's all right with me.

We'd heard from Joe [Brewer] about Ford's illness[2] in Paris and have been quite worried about him. And as I say I have been writing to you all every day since getting Joe's letter. How Ford is going to lose fifty pounds when he doesn't eat anything to speak of I can't see. I hope being made an LLD[3] was not too trying—I'd like to have seen Ford bending his head to accept the hood and "all its rights and privileges." We went over to Chapel Hill the other day to see Jim Boyd[4] get one and the procedure was very long drawn out.

Joe will have told you about our joint job[5] which we are still rather stunned over getting. The work will be a little heavier next year but this term it's been miraculously light—Allen has had all his mornings to himself and that has given him a chance to finish the novel. I haven't done any work except reading for a pioneer novel[6] but I was due to lay off work for a while anyhow.

You didn't say how Ford's history[7] was coming on? I've been thinking it might be finished by this time.

You knew Katherine Anne was married to Albert Erskine, business manager of the Southern Review, didn't you? We're still trying to take it in. She announced the news quite casually in a letter, on the heels of a long discussion of how she hated radios. Albert's a nice lad but he is still quite a lad and will be for years to come. It all beats me. Andrew has just been married to a girl from Memphis[8]—former pupil of Allen's at Southwestern. That also beats me.

Can't think of any other news. Where will you all be this summer? And will you be at Olivet for the conference and how are things going in general?

Love, from Caroline

Cornwall, Connecticut

1. Celebrated Congregational minister and lecturer (1813–1887).
2. Ford had had a serious heart attack.
3. Ford was made a Litt. D. at Olivet on June 19, 1938.
4. James Boyd, North Carolina–based novelist; his two major novels, *Drums* (1925) and *Marching On* (1927) are set in Revolutionary and Civil War times, respectively.
5. The Tates were teaching at the Woman's College of the University of North Carolina in Greensboro as of spring term 1938.
6. *Green Centuries* (1941).
7. Ford finished *The March of Literature* on July 12, 1938; the book was published in October. Gordon here refers to a missing letter from Biala.
8. Andrew Lytle married Edna Barker on June 20, 1938.

CG 40. CG to JB. TLS. 1 l. [July 1938] West Cornwall.

WEST CORNWALL, Conn.

Dear Janice:

I am so glad the ms turned up. I felt sure it was in that spot but it was a relief to get my hands on it. We stayed only a few days at Merry Mont and went to Benfolly only once. I've never seen the place look so nice. It's been the wettest season we ever had and the whole hill was green, right up to the brick porch. K. A. and I gathered hollyhock seeds from half a dozen states on our way home from Michigan last year. I sowed them around the brick porch and they're as tall as saplings. And the Normans had dozens of chickens all ready to fry—of course the earth would give forth its fruits the very year we're away.

We are settled in a dilapidated farm house about three miles from the Mark Van Dorens' place. There is no confort moderne—except one tap in the kitchen. The house is all settled over to one corner and shakes every time you walk. The beds are hard, the bedrooms the size of pocket handkerchiefs. However it's just the kind of house we both work in and we're enjoying it—or will enjoy it when things calm down a little. Allen has been in the throes of finishing his novel [*The Fathers*] and has been getting up at five and working all day long. I don't believe even Ford could show more industry. I suppose they have been neck and neck on their books these last few weeks. But Ford must have come under the wire first, it being now past the fourteenth. (I never doubt that he will finish his book on the very date he set.) God, it must be a relief to have it over!

About that picture: I can only repeat what I told you at Olivet: I will never forgive you if you missed a sale. I like it very much but no more than some other of your pictures. When I mentioned buying it I thought there was an extra hundred dollars on hand but when I got to the family exchequer I found Allen had beat me to it, withdrawing the hundred to repay Andrew a long standing debt. I have felt for some time that I ought to be able to hand myself a handsome present and cannot think of anything I'd rather have than one of your pictures but so far have never had my hands on an extra hundred or even twenty five—it has taken at least half the salary to pay off pressing debts. Earle Balch was here yesterday and reported that the advance sale on The Fathers was five thousand already. We made a great hurrah until we realized that that just paid back the advance. However when you're in a hole it's a comfort to get your head even with the earth and I'm hoping that next year we may not only be out of debt but have a little extra money.

Love to you both and congratulations to Ford on finishing his book,

Caroline

CG 41. TLS. 2 ll. [Oct. 1938] Greensboro.

Dear Ford:

I have had such a grand time with your book [*The March of Literature*]! It is a delight to read. You have done the seemingly impossible thing—written an outline history that is a real book. Nobody else but you could have done it. It is a real feat. I've read every word of the book but I'll be reading it again and again. It's a godsend to me in my classes. I can't adopt it as a text book—our girls are too poor. But they're clubbing together and buying it in groups of twos and threes and I've put as many copies in the library as they'd stand for. And Allen and I are spreading the good word around at Chapel Hill too. (That's the main concern. Ours is the Woman's branch of the college, sometimes inelegantly referred to as the W. C. of U. N. C.)

We spent the summer in Connecticut in a hundred year old house which we rented from the niece of H. Beecher Stowe.[1] There was only one water tap in the whole house—the kitchen sink. We cooked on an enormous wood stove and pumped our own water with a gasoline pump. But it was all so much easier than Benfolly that we never regretted our choice. Allen started working the second day we got there and finished his novel in the middle of July.[2] He wrote fifteen pages one day. Towards the last he said his people woke him up in the mornings talking—the ultimate desideratum of every novelist, I suppose.

I am wondering where and how you both are. Will you stay in New York this winter or are you going back to France? I rather hope you won't start on another great work right away. You must be terribly tired after that stupendous effort. I don't yet see how even you managed to write such a tome in such a short time, working as constantly as I know you did.

I have been trying to start my new novel [*Green Centuries*] for a week now, suffering the way one suffers on such occasions. Sunday before last I went down to Salisbury and picked the exact spot where my family are going to live. It is at the "Trading Ford" on the Yadkin river. The Great Trading Path which ran from New England to South Carolina crosses the river here. I was armed with a description an eighteenth century traveller had written of the place. He says "This most pleasant river may be something broader than the Thames at Kingston and with its warbling makes a reverberating sound upon its bright marble rocks. It is beautified by a continuos train of swans and other waterfowl . . . the pleasantest spot in the western world. Nor could all

Europe afford a pleasanter site were it inhabited by Christians and cultivated by ingenious hands . . ."

This pleasant spot is now inhabited by Christians and cultivated by some of the most ingenious hands in the western world. The Duke Power Company has its great power plant on the exact spot where the traders used to cross. The river is a horrid yellow. The land around looks red and raw as if it had been skinned. The contrast was so startling that when I discovered that this, this was Trading Ford for which I had searched so long I almost fell off the Duke Power turbine from which I was viewing the river. I aim to take a family from this place to the Watauga country in Tennessee and it is going to take some doing. I don't see how I can write the book in less than two years.

Allen is reviewing your book for John Ransom's new magazine, "The Kenyon Review." Have you had a letter from Ransom? He wrote us that he was going to ask you for an article. I hope you can write one for him. His new magazine ought to be very good. He will be in a situation to command the best work too. Unlike most quarterlies he is going to pay on acceptance and I think he will be able to pay a little more than the others do. The address is just The Kenyon Review, Kenyon, Ohio.

Manson Radford and his wife have moved from the Village and are living at 164 East Sixty Fourth street. Give them a ring. I know they will want to see you all.

We stopped in New York three days but saw hardly anybody. Leonie Adams and her husband were our neighbors in the country this summer. Leonie seems very happy married. Allen and I both liked Bill [Troy] very much.

Allen and Nancy send love. We have a new house this year, on the outskirts of town. It is a six room cottage which we rent for forty five dollars a month. With it goes a tremendous garden. Mimosa trees, pomegranate bushes, three fig trees and dozens of roses—I still cut great bunches every morning.

Write when you can. I do hope things are going well for you both,

as ever,
Caroline

The Woman's College,
Greensboro, North Carolina

I like your chapters on Fielding and Richardson[3] so much and I like too particularly the one on the Latin poets.

1. Harriet Beecher Stowe (1811–1896) spent her childhood in Connecticut;

later a visit to Kentucky inspired her to write her dramatically influential *Uncle Tom's Cabin* (1852).

2. *The Fathers* was published in September 1938.

3. Henry Fielding (1704–1754) and Samuel Richardson (1689–1761), the two great English novelists who contributed significantly to the establishment of the novel as a respected genre.

CG 42. CG to JB. TLS. 1 l. [End of June 1939] Monteagle.

Dearest Janice:

I have been writing to you and Ford for weeks—in my mind— but there has been no news to tell and we have all been working so hard I was too dull to write a letter. Then yesterday Andrew's wife came across the road with the news about Ford. I wish we could be with you. I am not even certain where you are. We got the news from an A.P. dispatch headed Deauville. I am wondering whether you had gone to Deauville.

I thought it was foolish of Ford to go back to France this summer but perhaps an instinct took him there. I am glad he died in France for he loved it so. After a while maybe we can all be glad that he died in the harness. I don't believe he could have stood growing old and not being able to work. I have wished these last few years that he didn't have to work so hard but it *is* a fine thing to be able to work right up to the last and God knows he did it.

I can't write a letter this morning. I am too upset. We all are— we really can't quite take it in yet.

We are cabling fifty dollars along with this message—just in chance it might be needed. When you can, please write and tell us your plans. We will be here at Monteagle until September when we will go to Princeton. If you are coming back to America you know that you will be welcomed at either place whenever it suits you to come to us. Love from all of us and I wish so very much that we could be with you to help,

as always,
Caroline

Monteagle, Tennessee

Index of Names and Titles

Abbott, Jacob, 50
Adams, Léonie, xvii, xxii, 58, 80, 82, 103, 109
Agar, Eleanor, 65
Agar, Herbert, 65, 97
Aleck Maury, Sportsman (Gordon), xvii, xxv–xxvi, 57, 62, 65, 66, 67, 70, 72, 73, 74, 76, 77, 78, 80
Allen, Hervey, 88
Alliott, Jeanne, 27, 33
Ancestors in Exile (Tate), 52, 55, 58
Anderson, Sherwood, 97
Anthony Adverse (Allen), 88
"As I Like It" (Phelps), 61
Asch, Nathan, 12, 26, 80, 83, 88
Atterbury, Walter, 98
Avent, Jim, 75–76

"B from Bull's Foot" (Gordon and Buckingham), 73, 81
Baker, Dorothy, 10
Baker, Howard, 9
Balch, Earle, 78, 107
Bandler, Bernard, 22, 24, 34, 35
Bandy, Alice, 9
Bandy, William O., 9
Beecher, Henry Ward, 105
Beiderbecke, Bix, 10
Biala, Janice: as artist, xxi, xxiii, xxiv, xxvi, xxvii, xxxi, xxxiiin 22, xxxvi,
13, 18, 25, 28, 41, 48, 54, 56, 66, 68, 69, 76, 77, 78, 79, 85, 95, 96, 98, 102, 107; contributions by, in Ford's letters, 15, 27–28, 56, 60–61; letter to, after Ford's death, xxix, 110; mentioned, xviii–xxxvi, 14–106
Bird, William, 9
Bishop, John Peale, 18, 39, 70
Bishop, Margaret, 39, 70
Blume, Peter, 49
Bogan, Louise, 53–54, 55
Bon Gaultier. *See* Martin, Theodore
Bowen, Stella, xii, xvi, xvii, xxiii, xxiv, xxxi, xxxvi, 27, 33, 38, 42, 43, 48, 54, 59
Boyd, James, 106
Boyden, Polly Chase, xix, 9
Brace, Donald, 61
Bradley, William A., 48, 61
Brande, Dorothea, 87, 92
Brandt, Zelma C., 72
Brave New World (Huxley), 61
Brewer, Joseph, xxviii, 91, 92, 93, 95, 105, 106
Brown, Susan Jenkins, xx, 4, 5, 8, 11, 88
Brown, William Slater, 11, 88, 90
Brown Owl, The (Ford), xi

Brustlein, Daniel, xxix, xxxiiin 22
Buckingham, Nash, 81
"Buckshee" (Ford), 26

Cabell, James Branch, 18
Campbell, Margaret (Pidie)
    Meriwether, 16, 32, 38, 43, 89, 98
Campbell, Paul, 98
Cantos of Ezra Pound, The: Some
    Testimonies (ed. Ford), xxv, 51
"Captive, The" (Gordon), 19, 20, 21
"Caroline Gordon" [Homage to
    Ford in New Directions]
    (Gordon), xxx
Caroline Gordon (Makowsky),
    xxxiiin 15
Caroline Gordon (Stuckey), xxxiiin
    9
"Caroline Gordon, Ford Madox
    Ford" (Core), xxxiin 2
"Caroline Gordon's Golden Ball"
    (Ross), xxxivn 35
Cash, Harold, 95, 97, 100, 103
Cato, Marcus Porcius, 68
Cézanne, Paul, 68
Cheatham, Elizabeth, xvi, xvii
Chicuelo, 68
Chipper, Richard, 55
Close Connections (Waldron), xxxii–
    xxxiiin 6, xxxivn 34
Collected Poems (Ford), 90
Collins, Seward, 21, 25, 48, 49, 87, 92
Compleat Angler, The (Walton), 57
"Conference on Literature and
    Reading" (Cutrer), xxxiiin 28
"Contrasts: Memories of John
    Galsworthy and George Moore"
    (Ford), xxv, 45, 47
Core, Deborah, xxxiin 2
Correspondence of Ford Madox Ford
    and Stella Bowen, The (ed. Stang
    and Cochran), xxxiin 3
Cowley, Malcolm, 11, 18, 34, 50, 51,
    52, 58, 88
Cowley, Peggy, 11, 18
Cranford (Gaskell), 97
Crowe, Helen, 9, 27, 39, 43
Cup of Fury, The (Gordon). See
    None Shall Look Back
Cutrer, Thomas W., xxxiiin 28

Dark Laughter (Anderson), 97
Dashiell, Alfred, 75
Davidson, Donald, 48
Davis, George, 12
Davis, Jefferson, xv–xvi
Day, Dorothy, 10
Dickson, Lovat, 56, 76, 77
Doc, Uncle, 47, 48, 58–60
Douglas, Norman, 12
Draft of XXX Cantos, A (Pound),
    xxv, 51
Draper, Muriel, 34
Draper, Paul, 34
Dreiser, Theodore, xxvi
Drums (Boyd), 106
Dubliners (Joyce), 79
Dudley, Nick, 47
Durant, M., 37

Eggleston, Edward, 100
"Elegy Written in a Country
    Churchyard, An" (Gray), 17
"Elephant, The" (Gordon), xxx–xxxi
Eliot, T. S., xxv, 58, 60
Erskine, Albert, 106
Exile's Return (Cowley), 50, 58
"Ezra" (Ford), xiv

Fathers, The (Tate), 36, 52, 97, 98,
    100, 105, 106, 107, 108
Faulkner, William, 21–22, 35, 43
Ferguson, Molly, 32
Fielding, Henry, 109
Fifth Queen, The (Ford), xi, xx
Firman/Furman, 4–5, 8
Fitzgerald, F. Scott, xvii
"Fixed Abode, A" (Gordon), xxxii
Fixx, Calvin, xiv
Flannery O'Connor and Caroline
    Gordon (comp. Golden and
    Sullivan), xxxivn 32
Flaubert, Gustave, xxx
"Fleuve Profond" (Ford), 26
Ford, Julie, xvii, xxiv, xxxvi, 8, 9, 11,
    13, 20, 27, 28, 29, 30, 38, 43, 54, 60
Ford Madox Ford (Saunders), xvi,
    xxxiiin 10
"Ford Madox Ford and the Baton
    Rouge Writers' Conference"
    (Webb), xxxiiin 28

"From Ford Madox Ford" (Ford),
   xxv, 51
Frost, Ed, 58
"Funeral in Town" (Gordon), xviii

Galsworthy, John, xxv, 46
Garden of Adonis, The (Gordon), 18,
   19, 35, 45, 49, 55, 57, 60, 98, 103
Gaskell, Elizabeth Cleghorn, 97
Gau, Mme, 11, 33–34
Gilman, Coburn, 34, 72
Glasgow, Ellen, 18, 21
Golden, Robert E., xxxivn 32
Goldring, Douglas, xiv
Goldsmith, Alfred, 56
Gone With the Wind (Mitchell), 88,
   89
Good Soldier, A (Gordon), xxxi
Good Soldier, The (Ford), xi, xv
Gordon, James Maury Morris, xii,
   xix, xxi, xxv, 5, 9, 32, 57, 60, 70
Gorman, Herbert, xii
Gorman, Jean Wright, xii
Gray, Thomas, 17
Great Trade Route (Ford), 95, 98, 99
Green, Paul, 21
Green Centuries (Gordon), xxxi,
   106, 108–9
Guggenheim, Peggy, 12
Guinzberg, Harold, 8

"Happy Farmers" (Ransom), 82
Hardy, Thomas, 81
Harris, Ruth, 36, 37, 38
Harrison, Barbara, 27
Hauptmann, Bruno, 31
Hemingway, Clarence E., xiv
Hemingway, Ernest, xvii, xxv, 15, 21
Henry, Gustavus Adolphus (Gus), 17
Henry VIII, xi
Henry for Hugh (Ford), 53, 60, 68,
   69, 72
Herbst, Josephine, xiii, 52, 72
Hersch, Lee, 12
Hersch, Virginia, 12
History of Our Own Times, A
   (Ford), 4, 7
Holden, Raymond, 53–54
Hoosier Schoolmaster, The
   (Eggleston), 100

House of Fiction, The (ed. Gordon
   and Tate), 78
Howard, Katharine, xi
Howe, W. T. H., 56, 60, 62, 63
Hueffer, Elsie Martindale, xvii,
   xviii, xxxiiin 12
Hueffer, Francis, xi
Hughes, Jim, 10
Hunt, Violet, xvii, xxvi
Huxley, Aldous, 59

I Have This to Say (Hunt), xxvi
Iliad, xxvii
"Immortal Woman, The" (Tate), 35
In Abraham's Bosom (Green), 23
It Was the Nightingale (Ford), 53, 56,
   57, 60, 61, 64–65

Jackson, Stonewall (Thomas J.), xv
James, Henry, xxx, 24, 30, 53, 85
Jarrell, Randall, 79
Jeanne, Mme. *See* Alliott, Jeanne
Jefferson Davis, His Rise and Fall
   (Tate), xv–xvi
Jenkins, Susan. *See* Brown, Susan
   Jenkins
Jones, Jefferson, 61, 72
Jonza, Nancylee Novell, xxxivn 30
Joyce, James, xxv, 79
Jungle Ways (Seabrook), 15

*Katherine Anne Porter's French Song
   Book* (Porter), 30
Kerr, Ruth, 5, 7–8
Kirstein, Lincoln, 24

Lake, Eileen, 71, 73, 74
Lake, Michael, 67, 71, 73, 74
Lalanda, 68
Lamure, Gisette, 35, 37, 49, 54
Lanier, Lyle, 31, 34
Lanier, Mannie (Chink), 31, 34
"Last Day in the Field, The"
   (Gordon), 74
Last Post (Ford), xiv, xv
"Latin Quarter" (Ford), 90
Lee, Robert E., xxiii, 20
Letters of Ford Madox Ford (ed.
   Ludwig), xxxiiin 27, 57
Lewisohn, Ludwig, 70

Life and Passion of Alexander Maury, The (Gordon). *See Aleck Maury, Sportsman*

Life on the Mississippi (Twain), 83

Lindbergh, Charles A., 31

Little Less than Gods, A (Ford), xv

Loeb, Harold, xx, 12

Loewe, Julia M. *See* Ford, Julie

Long, Ray, 27, 29, 53, 54

Loving, Pierre, 34

Lowell, Robert, xxviii, xxx

Lowenfels, Lillian, 43, 67

Lowenfels, Walter, 40, 41, 43, 67

Lowes, Marvin McCord, 82

Lytle, Andrew, xiii, xxvii, xxix, xxxv, 21, 47, 50, 62, 79, 84, 89, 92, 93, 97, 99, 102, 106

Lytle, Edna Barker, xxix, 106, 110

Lytle, Polly, 84, 89

Lytle, Robert Logan, 47, 50, 84, 89, 92, 93, 99–100

Lytle-Tate Letters, The (ed. Young and Sarcone), xxxiiin 19

Macauley, Robie, xxix

Makowsky, Veronica A., xvii–xviii

March of Literature, The (Ford), 96, 106, 107, 108, 109

Marching On (Boyd), 106

Marie of Roumania, Queen, 70

Marmion (Scott), 23

Martin, Theodore, 54

Martindale, Elsie. *See* Hueffer, Elsie Martindale

McIntosh, Mary, 5, 9, 28

McLean, Vance, 56, 57, 59, 60, 62

"Mediterranen, The" (Tate), xxiii, xxvi, 75

Mediterranen and Other Poems, The (Tate), xxvi, 84

Memoirs and Opinions (Tate), xvi, xvii

Memoirs of a Fox-Hunting Man (Sassoon), 65

Meriwether, Caroline Ferguson, xii, 19–20, 46, 47, 49, 62, 75

Meriwether, Loulie, 48, 57, 58–59

Meriwether, Marion (Manny), 62

Meriwether, Robert Emmet, 17

Mitchell, Margaret, 88

Mizener, Arthur, xii, xiii, xv

Modern American Poetry (ed. Untermeyer), 33

Moe, Henry Allen, 20, 41, 45, 46, 48

Monk, Samuel, 97

Moore, Virginia, 44, 65

Morning's Favour, A (Gordon). *See Garden of Adonis, The*

Most Beautiful Lady (Brande), 87, 92

Munson, Gorham B., 58

Murphy, Richard, 29

Myrick, Mrs., 83

New York Is Not America (Ford), xiv

Ney, Michel, xv

None Shall Look Back (Gordon), xxvii, 75, 83, 84, 85, 88, 89, 90, 92, 94, 98, 99, 101, 104

Norman, Mr., 19, 65, 69, 89, 102, 107

Notterdam (Ford). *See When the Wicked Man*

Of Time and the River (Wolfe), 76, 79

"Old Mrs. Llewellyn" (Gordon), xv

"Old Red" (Gordon), xxiv–xxv, 41, 58, 60

"Olive Garden, The" (Gordon), xxx

"One More Time" (Gordon), 74

Opening of a Door, The (Davis), 12

Ouida. *See* Ramée, Marie Louise de la

Parade's End (Ford), xi, xv, xx, xxix, xxx, xxxi, 96

Pastellière, M. le Vicome de la, 35, 68

Pastellière, Mme la Vicomtesse de la, 35, 37, 38

Pats, the. *See* Pastellière, de la

Penhally (Gordon), xviii, xix, xx–xxi, xxv, 3, 4, 7, 9, 10, 13–14, 15, 16–17, 18, 19, 21, 24, 26, 30, 45, 55, 58, 75

Perkins, Maxwell, xix, xxv, xxxvi, 14, 16, 17, 18, 21, 45, 62, 65, 75, 76, 78, 79, 81, 88–89, 98, 104

Perry, Mr., 10

Personae (Pound), xiv

Phelps, William Lyon, 60, 70

"Picnic at Cassis" (Tate). *See*
    "Mediterranean, The"
Pity Is Not Enough (Herbst), 52
Porter, Katherine Anne, xiii, xiv,
    xvi, xix, xxii, xxiii, xxiv, xxxvi, 10,
    18, 22, 24, 27, 28, 30, 33, 39, 41, 42,
    43, 47, 49, 52, 55, 56, 58, 61, 66, 90,
    106, 107
Portraits from Life (Ford), 96, 101
Pound, Ezra, xiv, xxi, xxii, xxv, 51
Pound/Ford (ed. Lindberg-
    Seyersted), xxxiin 5
Pressly, Eugene, xxii, xxiii, xxxv, 39,
    41, 42, 47, 49, 52, 55, 58, 60, 61, 66
Provence (Ford), xxvi, 65, 68, 69, 71,
    74, 77, 78, 79, 81, 83
Putnam, Phelps, 18, 44, 46, 48
Putnam, Una, 20, 48

Radford, Manson, 62, 65, 77, 81,
    100, 109
Radford, Rose, 77, 81, 100, 109
Ramée, Marie Louise de la (pseud.
    Ouida), 21
Ransom, John Crowe, 19, 31, 58, 79,
    82, 100, 109
Rash Act, The (Ford), 13, 29, 30, 32,
    54
*Reactionary Essays on Poetry and
    Ideas* (Tate), 85
Return to Yesterday (Ford), 8, 13, 24,
    26, 60
[Review of *Henry for Hugh*]
    (Gordon), 69, 72
[Review of *None Shall Look Back*]
    (Ford), xxvii, 98
Richardson, Samuel, 109
Rives, Amélie (Princess
    Troubetzkoy), 21
Road in Search of America, The
    (Asch), 80
Robertson, Andrewena, 93
Robertson, Mr., 84, 92
Rorty, James, 83
Ross, Danforth, xxxivn 35
Ross, Dorothy Ann, 33
Rossetti, Christina, xi, xvi

Saddest Story, The (Mizener), xii
Sanborn, Herbert, 86

Sanctuary (Faulkner), 43
Sassoon, Siegfried, 65
Saunders, Max, xvi, xxxivn 33, 26
Sawyer, Mrs., 54
Sawyer, Warren, 54, 61
Scott, Walter, 23
Seabrook, Katie, 36
Seabrook, William B., 12–13, 17, 26,
    27, 36
"Secret of the Captain, The"
    (Tate). *See* "To the
    Lacedemonians"
Sedgwick, Ellery, 45
Seldes, George, 12, 26
Ship of Fools (Porter), 20
Smith, Harrison, 22
Smith, John, 44
Smith, Richard R., 53, 54
Smith, T. R., 27
So Red the Rose (Young), 59, 66, 78
South Lodge (Goldring), xiv
South Wind (Douglas), 12
Southern Mandarins, The (ed.
    Wood), xxxiiin 14
Sportsman's Sketches, A (Turgenev),
    xxv, 73
Stafford, Jean, xxx
"Stage in American Literature, A"
    (Ford), xx–xxi, 21, 24, 25
Starched Blue Sky of Spain, The
    (Herbst), xiii
Stein, Gertrude, xvii, 43
Stick-Up, The (Loving), 34
Stonewall Jackson, the Good Soldier
    (Tate), xv
"Story of Ford Madox Ford, The"
    (Gordon), xxx
Stowe, Harriet Beecher, 108
Stuckey, W. J., xxxiiin 9
Sullivan, Mary C., xxxivn 32
"Summer Dust" (Gordon), xviii, 10
Sun Also Rises, The (Hemingway), 15

Taggard, Genevieve, 90
Tate, Allen. *See Ancestors in Exile,
    Fathers, The, House of Fiction, The,*
    "Immortal Woman, The,"
    Jefferson Davis, "Mediterranean,
    The," *Mediterranean and Other
    Poems, The, Memoirs and Opin-*

Tate, Allen, *cont.*
  *ions, Reactionary Essays, Stonewall
  Jackson,* "To the Lacedemonians,"
  Turn of the Screw, The; men-
  tioned, xii–xxxv, 7–109
Tate, Ben, xix
Tate, Nancy, xii, xvii, xxxvi, 9, 10, 11,
  13, 20, 22, 30, 31, 32, 33–34, 35, 43,
  46, 52, 55, 60, 62, 66, 70, 80, 84, 85,
  89, 90, 94, 98, 102, 103, 104, 109
"Techniques" (Ford), 83
Thackeray, William Makepeace, 88
"That Evening Sun" (Faulkner), 22
"To Cumberland" (Gordon). *See*
  "Captive, The"
"To Ford Madox Ford" (Gordon),
  xxx
"To the Lacedemonians" (Tate), 33
"To Thy Chamber Window,
  Sweet" (Gordon), 74
Toklas, Alice B., 43
Tolstoy, Lev Nikolayevich, xxvii
"Tom Rivers" (Gordon), 41
Trask, Mary. *See* McIntosh, Mary
Trask, Willard, 5, 9, 28, 32
Trollope, Anthony, 97
Troy, William, 58, 82, 103, 109
Turgenev, Ivan, xxv, 73
"Turn of the Screw, The" (James),
  85
Turn of the Screw, The (Tate), 85
Twain, Mark, 83
Tworkov, Jack, 54, 76
Tworkov, Wally, xxviii, 102, 103, 104

Uncle Doc. *See* Doc, Uncle
Uncle Tom's Cabin (Stowe), 110
Underground Stream, The (Jonza),
  xxxivn 30
Untermeyer, John, 43, 44
Untermeyer, Louis, 32–33

Van Dine, S. S. *See* Wright,
  Willard Huntington

Van Doren, Carl, 88
Van Doren, Dorothy, 88
Van Doren, Irita, 88
Van Doren, Mark, 17, 88
Vanity Fair (Thackeray), 88

Wake Up and Live (Brande), 87, 92
Waldron, Ann, xxxii–xxxiiin 6
Waller, James, 85
Walsh, Tom, 77
Walton, Izaak, 57
Warren, Cinina, 19, 22, 24, 62, 65,
  74, 75
Warren, Robert Penn, xiii, xvi,
  xxxvi, 11, 19, 22, 24, 62, 64, 65, 74,
  75, 79, 82, 90
Webb, Max, xxxiiin 28
Wescott, Glenway, xiv
Wheeler, Monroe, 28
"When the Light Gets Green"
  (Warren), 79
When the Wicked Man (Ford), 4–5,
  8, 10, 13, 22
Who Owns America, 58, 66, 86
Wilds, Catherine, 47, 49, 95, 97,
  100–101, 103
Williams, Gus, 17–18
Winters, Yvor, xviii
Wodehouse, P. G., 64
Wolfe, Thomas, 76, 79
Wood, Nancy Tate. *See* Tate,
  Nancy
Wood, Sally, xvi, xix, xxi, xxii, xxxvi,
  33, 35, 63
Wright, Cecil, 40, 54, 61, 63
Wright, Margaret, 54, 61
Wright, Rene, xvi, xvii, 22
Wright, Willard Huntington
  (pseud. S. S. Van Dine), 71

Young, Stark, 58, 66, 78
Young Man with a Horn (Baker,
  Dorothy), 10